T0125058

Martin Nicholas Kunz . Patricia Massó

best | designed

affordable hotels

avedition

01 02

Design or not design—that is the question; or more precisely, the choice that globe trotters faced in the past. Those lacking in spare change had to pass by the beautiful luxury hotels and put up, in every sense of the word, with cookie-cutter budget accommodations. In the meantime, creative hoteliers have recognised the need for affordable design hotels. What began as an apparent niche market has developed into the tourism success story of recent years. Especially the large international target group has primarily contributed to the success of the new concepts. Business travelers in their mid-forties who are on the road quite a bit for professional reasons are just as much a part of this group as young families who expect more from their holidays than the package hotel. There are also 28-year olds who, after successfully completing their studies, spend their money on trendy furnishings and the latest fashion clothing. Thus, it is natural that they would want to also spend their holidays in an atmosphere that corresponds to their personal style. All of these people are extremely mobile and cosmopolitan. They think globally and select their destinations according to personal interests and not based on whether these destinations are next door or on another continent. The individuals in this target group are well aware of what they are worth, and what design is worth. For them, inexpensive does not mean cheap, and a good value means that certain things are worth their value. In the architecturally-focused hotels in the categories they can afford, prices are around 200 euros per night, and sometimes much less. At first glance, it still seems like a great deal of money, but travelers know exactly what awaits them and what they can expect for their money. In addition to classic service and excellent furnishings,

03 04

one feature is of central importance to them: individuality. Each hotel in this book is based on a concept that works exclusively at that particular location and nowhere else. After all, the architecture determines the furnishings and the location the atmosphere. Thus, each hotel is unique. It challenges its guests and sends them on expeditions of discovery. Visitors definitely will not suffer from déjà vu. Guests feel that their lifestyles are understood, not lastly because the makers themselves come from the same target group. They are creative and open, and let their personality flow into their creative process. It is

their ambition that surprises and excites guests with unusual ideas. Proof of their success is provided on the following pages.

01 | The Farmer's Daughter

02 | Hotel QT

03 | Hotel on Rivington

04 | Hotel V

05 06

Design oder nicht sein. Vor diesen beiden Möglichkeiten standen Globetrotter in der Vergangenheit. Wem das nötige Kleingeld fehlte, der musste die wunderschönen Luxushotels links an der Straße liegen lassen und in austauschbaren Budget-Unterkünften im wahren Sinn des Wortes absteigen. Mittlerweile haben findige Hoteliers den Bedarf an günstigen Designhäusern erkannt. Der vermeintliche Nischenmarkt hat sich zu der touristischen Erfolgsgeschichte der letzten Jahre entwickelt. Zum Erfolg der neuen Konzepte trägt vor allem die große internationale Zielgruppe bei.

Geschäftsleute Mitte 40, die aus beruflichen Gründen viel unterwegs sind, gehören genauso dazu, wie junge Familien, die von ihrem Urlaub mehr erwarten als das Pauschalhotel bietet. Es sind auch 28-Jährige, die nach erfolgreichem Studium ihr Geld für eine schicke Einrichtung und angesagte Mode ausgeben. Klar, dass sie sich auch im Urlaub in einem Umfeld bewegen möchten, das ihrem persönlichen Stil entspricht. All diese Menschen sind extrem mobil und kosmopolitisch. Sie denken global und wählen das Reiseziel nach persönlichen Interessen, nicht danach, ob es nebenan oder

auf einem anderen Kontinent liegt. Dabei weiß diese Zielgruppe genau, was sie sich selbst und was das Design wert ist. Günstig heißt für sie nicht billig. Preiswert heißt eben, dass bestimmte Dinge ihren Preis wert sind. In der für sie in Frage kommenden Kategorie der architekturbetonten Hotels liegt dieser Preis um die 200 Euro pro Nacht, manchmal aber auch weit darunter. Auf den ersten Blick immer noch viel Geld, doch die Reisenden wissen genau, was sie dafür erwarten und was sie erwarten können. Neben klassischen Serviceangeboten und einer hervorragenden Ausstattung, steht

07 08

vor allem ein Punkt im Zentrum des Interesses: Individualität. Jedes Hotel in diesem Buch basiert auf einem Konzept, dass nur an diesem einen Ort genauso und nicht anders funktioniert. Schließlich bedingt die Architektur die Einrichtung und der Ort die Atmosphäre. So ist jedes Haus einzigartig. Es fordert seine Gäste heraus und schickt sie auf eine Entdeckungsreise. Das „Alles schon gesehen"-Gefühl tritt garantiert nicht ein. Die Besucher fühlen sich in ihrem Lebensstil verstanden. Nicht zuletzt, weil die Macher selbst oft direkt aus der Zielgruppe kommen. Sie sind kreativ, weltoffen und haben ihre Persönlichkeit

mit in die Gestaltung einfließen lassen. Ihr Ergeiz ist es, die Gäste mit ungewöhnlichen Ideen zu überraschen und zu begeistern. Davon, dass ihnen das gelungen ist, kann man sich auf den folgenden Seiten überzeugen.

05 | Enterprise Hotel

06 | United Hotel

07 | Theoxenia

08 | Caravanserai

b+b belgravia | london . great britain
DESIGN: Lynne Reid

Visitors to London can hardly escape the charm of the city's typical, rambling townhouses. However, everyone can do without clattering doors, antiquated bathrooms and draughty windows. That is just what Penny Brown, Lynne Reid and Colette Huck thought when they were planning their own Bed and Breakfast. They were so successful at imbuing the classic British concept with a modern atmosphere that, just one year after the opening in 2004, they were named the Best Bed and Breakfast in London by the renowned Eurostar Visit London Awards. The center of the building is the large, bright lounge with a fireplace, in which guests meet to read the newspaper and drink tea. Due to circumstances surrounding the house's history, the 17 rooms are small, yet their large windows and optimal room utilization prevent them from feeling confining. Dark woods combined with light fabrics create a timelessly elegant look. In addition to design, personal contact to guests is one of the concept's pillars. For instance, breakfast is prepared in front of the guests in the open kitchen. In addition, the owners are happy to share their personal, favorite fashion and dining addresses in Britain's capital.

Dem Charme, den die typischen verwinkelten Stadthäuser Londons ausüben, kann sich kaum ein Besucher der Stadt entziehen. Auf klappernde Türen, uralte Badezimmer und zugige Fenster kann dafür aber jeder verzichten. Das haben sich auch Penny Brown, Lynne Reid und Colette Huck gedacht, als sie ihr eigenes Bed and Breakfast planten. Das klassisch britische Konzept in modernem Ambiente umzusetzen, gelang ihnen so gut, dass sie bereits ein Jahr nach der Eröffnung 2004 als bestes Bed and Breakfast Londons bei den renommierten Eurostar Visit London Awards ausgezeichnet wurden. Das Zentrum des Hauses bildet die großzügige, helle Lounge mit Kamin, in der sich die Gäste zum Zeitungslesen und Teetrinken treffen. Die 17 Zimmer sind aufgrund der Gegebenheiten des historischen Gebäudes zwar klein, wirken aber durch die großen Fenster und die optimale Nutzung des Raums nicht eng. Dunkle Hölzer sorgen in Kombination mit hellen Stoffen für eine zeitlos elegante Optik. Neben dem Design gehört vor allem der persönliche Kontakt zum Gast zu den Grundpfeilern des Konzepts. So wird auch das Frühstück in der offenen Küche vor den Gästen zubereitet. Außerdem verraten die Eigentümerinnen gerne ihre persönlichen modischen und kulinarischen Lieblingsadressen in der britischen Hauptstadt.

01 | The lounge is the starting point for a shopping spree in the city's exclusive Belgravia district.

Die Lounge ist der Ausgangspunkt für eine Shopping-Tour im exklusiven Stadtteil Belgravia.

02 03

02 | Heavy curtains, patterned wallpaper and dark carpets have given way to clear, light designs.

Schwere Vorhänge, gemusterte Tapeten und dunkle Teppiche sind einem klaren, hellen Design gewichen.

03 | During the renovation of the old townhouse, care was taken to use every centimeter optimally.

Bei der Renovierung des alten Stadthauses wurde darauf geachtet, dass jeder Zentimeter optimal genutzt wird.

04 | The owners are already considering implementing their hotel concept on an international level as well.

Die Eigentümerinnen denken bereits darüber nach, ihr Hotelkonzept auch international umzusetzen.

04

hotel julien | antwerp . belgium

DESIGN: AID Architecten, Kristl Backermans, Mouche Van Hool

Just a short walk from the Cathedral of Our Lady, there is an elegantly modest little sign indicating the entrance to a jewel of a hotel. With only eleven rooms, it is divided into two buildings surrounding a courtyard that are narrow and high—typical for the architecture of the turn of the century. Almost every room is located on a different level, and no two floor plans are alike. For the architects, these were welcome conditions for individual design. For instance, guests have the choice between an airy attic suite with visible wooden beams and a round bathtub or the "Bürgerhaus" rooms. White or cream walls, light-colored fabrics, natural wooden floors, glass and premium yet modest furniture form the contemporary interior, which provides a contrast to the historical shell. The unusually large and sparkling-clean bathrooms consist of white marble and light-colored materials. The salon with woodcarvings and an open fireplace is a feast for the eyes, and, situated between the breakfast room and the courtyard patio that is open in summer, generates a living-room atmosphere. Of course, the generous breakfast buffet also includes that famous national specialty: Belgian chocolate.

Nur ein paar Schritte von der Liebfrauenkathedrale entfernt weist ein vornehm zurückhaltendes Schildchen auf den Eingang eines Hotel-Juwels hin. Seine nur elf Zimmer verteilen sich auf zwei, um einen Innenhof angeordnete Häuser, die – typisch für den Baustil der Jahrhundertwende – schmal und hoch sind. Fast jeder Raum befindet sich auf einer anderen Ebene und kein Grundriss gleicht dem anderen. Für die Architekten waren das willkommene Voraussetzungen zur individuellen Gestaltung. So hat man als Gast die Wahl zwischen der luftigen Dachgeschoß-Suite mit sichtbaren Holzbalken und runder Badewanne oder dem in weiß gehaltenen Bürgerhaus-Zimmern. Weiße oder cremfarbene Wände, helle Stoffe, naturbelassene Holzböden, Glas und eine edle aber reduzierter Möblierung stellen der historischen Hülle ein zeitgenössisches Interieur gegenüber. Die ungewöhnlich großen und blitzsauberen Bäder bestehen aus weißem Marmor und hellen Materialien. Eine Augenweide ist der Salon mit Holzschnitzereien und offenem Kamin, der zwischen dem Frühstücksraum und der im Sommer geöffneten Innenhofterrasse Wohnzimmeratmosphäre aufbringt. Das reichhaltige Frühstücksbüffet fährt natürlich auch die berühmte Spezialität des Landes auf: Belgische Schokolade.

14 | hotel julien

02 | Wooden furniture on antique floorboards generate atmosphere.
Holzmöbel auf alten Dielen schaffen Atmosphäre.

03 | Design classics are skillfully employed as style elements.
Designklassiker werden gekonnt als Stilelemente eingesetzt.

04 | A harmony of wood and glass.
Holz und Glas in Harmonie.

04

hotel v | amsterdam . netherlands

DESIGN: Mirjam Espinosa, Ronald Hooft Consulting

Amsterdam is a special city, and even those who do not wish to spend a lot of money there, should not have to stay in standart hotel. With this idea, the Hotel V was born. The hotel interior was designed and furnished by Mirjam Espinosa together with Dutch designer Ronald Hooft. In the process, they relied on natural materials and surprising contrasts. The fireplace in the lobby is set into a wall of pebbles, opposite a brilliantly violet sofa. In addition to scaled-down white tables and chairs, elements reminiscent of Africa are also apparent—gazelle antlers, fur pillows, unusual wooden stools. The carefully selected wall colors, from ocean blue to stone gray to pure white, enhance the individual effect of the decor. The V, opened in the year 2000, with its unmistakable design mix, strives to be an urban guesthouse that can compete with luxury accommodations. The hotel's goal is to capture the atmosphere and attitude of the Dutch capital without permanently exposing its guests to the hubbub of the metropolis. That is why it is located on the edge of the center. The fact that this concept is working is evident in the deliberation of its owners, who are seriously pondering a second establishment of this sort in Amsterdam.

Amsterdam ist eine besondere Stadt und auch wer dort nicht viel Geld ausgeben möchte, sollte nicht in einem x-beliebigen Hotel übernachten. Mit diesem Gedanken entstand das Hotel V. Das Hotel-Interieur wurde von Mirjam Espinosa zusammen mit dem niederländischen Designer Ronald Hooft entworfen und eingerichtet. Sie setzten dabei auf natürliche Materialien und überraschende Kontraste. Der Kamin in der Lobby ist in Kieselsteine eingefasst, ihm gegenüber steht ein leuchtend violettes Sofa. Neben reduzierten weißen Tischen und Stühlen fallen Elemente ins Auge, die an Afrika erinnern – ein Gazellengeweih, Fellkissen, außergewöhnliche Holzschemel. Die sorgfältig ausgewählten Wandfarben von Meeresblau über Steingrau bis zu Reinweiß unterstützen die individuelle Wirkung der Einrichtung. Das im Jahr 2000 eröffnete V will mit seinem unverwechselbaren Design-Mix ein urbanes Gästehaus sein, das klassischen Luxusunterkünften in nichts nachsteht. Ziel ist es, die Stimmung und das Lebensgefühl der niederländischen Hauptstadt einzufangen und zwar ohne, dass das Hotel seine Gäste permanent dem Rummel der Großstadt aussetzt. So liegt das Haus ganz bewusst am Rand des Zentrums. Dass dieses Konzept aufgeht, zeigen die Überlegungen der Macher, die intensiv über ein zweites Haus dieser Art in Amsterdam nachdenken.

01 | The V standard: A personal poem on the wall, fresh flowers on the table and something sweet on the pillow.

Der V Standard: Ein persönliches Gedicht an der Wand, frische Blumen auf dem Tisch und etwas Süßes auf dem Kopfkissen.

Specials
cafe latte   2,-
cappucino   2,-
espresso   2,-
fresh orange   2,50
juice
~~~~~~~~~~~   2,-
~ti   2,75
scrambled eggs
& toast   2,75
pastry of the day
& cappucino   3,50

02

03 04

02 | In the breakfast room, visitors from all over the world exchange their advice about Amsterdam.

Im Frühstücksraum tauschen Besucher aus aller Welt ihre Amsterdam-Tipps aus.

03 | 04 In their own rooms as in the entire house, guests can surf the Internet on their laptops thanks to wireless LAN.

Im eigenen Zimmer genau wie im gesamten Haus, können die Gäste dank Wireless LAN mit ihrem Laptop im Internet surfen.

stroom | rotterdam . netherlands
DESIGN: Gerben van der Molen from Stars Design

The fact that everything in Rotterdam is in flux is not only due to its location on the mouth of the Maas and Rhine flowing into the North Sea. The second-largest city in the Netherlands is also one of the cultural centers of the country. The Dutch are proud to have so much movement in their city. One symbol of this attitude is the Stroom, opened in 2005. The architecture of the hotel, comprising 18 studios, would be fair competition for any museum. Surprising views open up not only to passers-by but also to guests. For instance, they can look directly from the shower through a glass ceiling to the sky. However the view is even better from the roof-deck of the hotel. There is also a great deal to discover with regard to the furnishings. In Stroom, conventional perspectives have been discarded and rooms newly defined. In the process, architect Gerben van der Molen benefited from the fact that hardly any limits were set by the height and breadth of the former factory. His experiments do not even spare the sanctuary within every room—the bed. The Cocomat beds consist of four layers of specially-manufactured coconut fiber mats. Why shouldn't Caribbean dreams follows a typical Dutch day on a bicycle? After all, life is just one long river.

Dass in Rotterdam alles im Fluss ist, liegt nicht nur an der Lage an der Mündung von Maas und Rhein in die Nordsee. Die zweitgrößte Stadt der Niederlande gehört außerdem zu den kulturellen Zentren des Landes. Die Niederländer sind stolz darauf, dass sich in ihrer Stadt so viel bewegt. Ein Sinnbild für diese Einstellung ist das im Jahr 2005 eröffnete Stroom. Die Architektur des 18 Studios umfassenden Hotels macht jedem Museum Konkurrenz. Überraschende Perspektiven öffnen sich nicht nur Passanten von außen, sondern auch den Gästen von innen. Sie schauen zum Beispiel direkt von ihrer Dusche durch ein Glasdach in den Himmel. Noch besser ist der Ausblick allerdings von der Dachterrasse des Hotels. Auch was die Einrichtung betrifft, gibt es viel zu entdecken. Im Stroom werden gewohnte Perspektiven ausgehebelt und Räume neu definiert. Dabei kam Architekt Gerben van der Molen zugute, dass ihm in der ehemaligen Fabrik in punkto Höhe und Weite kaum Grenzen gesetzt waren. Seine Experimente machen selbst vor dem Heiligtum eines jeden Zimmers nicht halt – dem Bett. Die Cocomat-Betten bestehen aus vier Lagen speziell angefertigter Kokosfaser-Matten. Wieso sollten karibische Träume auch nicht auf einen typisch niederländischen Tag auf dem Fahrrad folgen? Schließlich ist das Leben doch ein einziger Fluss.

01 | The name says it all—Stroom is Dutch for "in the flow".

Der Name ist Programm - Stroom ist niederländisch für „im Fluss".

02 | The kitchen in the Stroom unites influences from all over the world, but of course true Dutch delights are avilable.

Die Küche im Stroom vereint Einflüsse aus aller Welt, echte niederländische Leckereien gib es natürlich auch.

03 | Beamer and DVD library ensure that even cozy evenings in your room are not boring.

Beamer und DVD-Bibliothek sorgen dafür, dass auch gemütliche Abende auf dem Zimmer nicht langweilig werden.

04 | In the studios, stairs lead up to the separate bedroom.

In den Studios führt eine Treppe zum separaten Schlafzimmer.

05 | If the bathroom in your own room isn't quite enough, you can get a massage in the hotel spa.

Wem das Bad im eigenen Zimmer nicht reicht, kann sich im Spa des Hauses massieren lassen.

25hours | hamburg . germany

DESIGN: Thomas Lau, Mark Hendrik Blieffert from HPV Hamburg; Evi Märklstetter, Armin Fischer from 3Meta

Almost all of the furniture here was created by up-and-coming designers. In the 89 rooms—in the sizes Small, Medium and Large—and three studios, hotel guests will find a colorful mix of simple lines and an homage to the Sixties and Seventies, with their bright colors and whimsical details. A further accent is the multifunctionality of the furnishings. For instance, the desk doubles as a bench or suitcase rest. The lobby, in which 420 chrome mirrors generate a kaleidoscope-like atmosphere, is bordered by the Tageswandel Bar. Nomen est omen: The "Changing Day" Bar, as the name implies, changes its appearance several times throughout the day via changes in the lighting and conversions to the bar area. The hotel's restaurant is called Esszimmer (Dining Room), and serves German and Italian cuisine. Right next to the restaurant, guests will find the lounge, which functions as a living room and invites visitors to relax by the fireplace or play a round of tabletop football. Business travelers can make use of two conference rooms for 25 and 60 participants.

Nahezu alle Möbel sind hier von jungen Designern entworfen. In den 89 Zimmern – in den Größen Small, Medium, Large – und drei Studios erwartet die Hotelgäste ein bunter Mix aus schlichter Linienführung und einer Hommage an die 60er und 70er Jahre mit kräftigen Farben und verspielten Details. Einen weiteren Akzent setzt die Multifunktionalität der Ausstattung. So lässt sich beispielsweise der Schreibtisch auch als Sitzgelegenheit oder Kofferablage nutzen. An die Lobby, in der 420 Chromspiegel eine kaleidoskopähnliche Atmosphäre erzeugen, schließt sich die Tageswandel Bar an. Nomen est omen: Die Bar verändert im Laufe des Tages mehrfach ihr Erscheinungsbild, indem die Beleuchtung wechselt und die Theke umgebaut wird. Das hauseigene Restaurant heißt Esszimmer und tischt deutsche und italienische Küche auf. Gleich nebenan befindet sich die Lounge, die als Wohnzimmer fungiert und zur Entspannung am Kamin oder zum Match am Kickertisch einlädt. Geschäftlich Reisenden stehen zwei Tagungsräume für 25 und 60 Teilnehmer zur Verfügung.

01 | Extravagant design characterizes the entire hotel.
Extravagantes Design kennzeichnet das gesamte Hotel.

02

03

02 | An eye for detail: Almost all furniture and accessories were created by up-and-coming designers.

Sinn fürs Detail: Fast alle Möbel und Accessoires wurden von Nachwuchsdesignern kreiert.

03 | Clear lines shape all hotel rooms.

Eine klare Linienführung prägt alle Hotelzimmer.

04 | Multifunctional: This desk doubles as a bench and suitcase rest.

Multifunktional: Dieser Schreibtisch ist zugleich Sitzgelegenheit und Kofferablage.

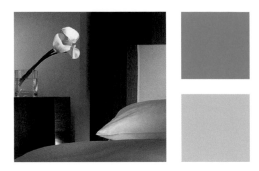

hopper st. antonius | cologne . germany
DESIGN: Rolf Kursawe

The hotel, constructed in 1904 in the direct vicinity of the cathedral and the main railway station, originally served as a journey men's home for the Kolping fraternity. In 1997, the building, called Antoniushaus and partially damaged in World War II, was renovated true to the original state and converted into a hotel. Behind the natural stone and clinker façade, guests will find a mixture of historical building fabric and contemporary design. High, vaulted ceilings and original Mettlach floor tiles in the restaurant, a historical stepped gable, antique ceiling joists and a cozy courtyard stand in contrast to the modern design of the 39 rooms and 15 suites. Here, precious materials such as teakwood, kambala wood, and marble are employed, as are furnishings including the latest in communications technology. Photographs by contemporary artists, to whose presentation and patronage the hotel is committed, contribute to the individual character of the rooms. A significant part of this collection was provided by the benefactor of the Photographic Collection of the Cologne Museum Ludwig and the co-founder of the Photokina exhibition, Professor L. Fritz Gruber. With his guidance, he supported the selection of the photos, supplied the contacts to the artists and, last but not least, is the namesake of the hotel's restaurant, the L. Fritz.

Das 1904 in unmittelbarer Nähe von Dom und Hauptbahnhof errichtete Gebäude beherbergte ursprünglich ein Gesellenheim der Kolping Bruderschaft. 1997 wurde das im Zweiten Weltkrieg teilweise beschädigte Antoniushaus originalgetreu saniert und zum Hotel umgestaltet. Hinter der Fassade aus Naturstein und Klinker findet sich eine Mischung aus historischer Bausubstanz und zeitgenössischem Design. Hohe gewölbte Decken und original Mettlacher Platten im Restaurant, ein historischer Treppengiebel, alte Deckenbalken und ein lauschiger Innenhof stehen in Kontrast zum modernen Design der 39 Zimmer und 15 Suiten. Hier finden sich edle Materialien wie Teakholz, Kambalaholz und Marmor neben einer Ausstattung mit neuester Kommunikationstechnik. Den individuellen Charakter der Räume bestimmen auch die Fotografien zeitgenössischer Künstler, zu deren Präsentation und Gönnerschaft sich das Hotel verschrieben hat. Maßgeblichen Anteil daran hat der Stifter der Fotografischen Sammlung des Kölner Museums Ludwig und Mitbegründer der Photokina, Professor L. Fritz Gruber. Er unterstützte beratend bei der Fotoauswahl, vermittelte die Kontakte zu den Künstlern und ist nicht zuletzt Namensgeber für das zum Hotel gehörende Restaurant, das L. Fritz.

01 | View from the foyer to the restaurant L. Fritz.
Blick vom Eingangsbereich in den Speisesaal des L. Fritz.

02 | Outdoor dining in the courtyard.

Speisen unter freiem Himmel im Innenhof.

03 | Advantageous downtown location with a view of the Cologne Cathedral.

Standortvorteil Innenstadt und Ausblick auf den Kölner Dom.

04 | Precious materials, design classics and photographic art in every room.

Edle Materialien, Design-Klassiker und Fotokunst in jedem Zimmer.

04

hotel bristol | frankfurt . germany

DESIGN: Oana Rosen

The history of this design hotel, just opened in 2003, is the history of a wondrous metamorphosis: Michael Rosen and Alex Urseanu transformed a run-of-the-mill, middle-class hotel into a place to be. Black and white dominate the lobby. Dark oak parquet, beige leather easy chairs, wenge-colored furniture and pleated lamps are further design elements. An extra-large mirror in the reception area has a counterpart in the Bristol Summer Lounge, an Asian-inspired garden with ponds, vine-covered walls and timber floorboards. The hotel owners have breathed new life into the old walls of the house: For instance, there is an extravagant lighting installation behind curtains. In the hallway leading from the lobby to the function rooms, showcases whose decoration is dedicated to varying themes, depending on the season or event, are built into the walls. In true cosmopolitan fashion, the hotel also boasts the elegant Bristol Bar, opened around the clock.

Die Geschichte des erst 2003 eröffneten Design Hotels ist die Geschichte einer wundersamen Verwandlung: Michael Rosen und Alex Urseanu gestalteten ein null-acht-fünfzehn Mittelklasse-Haus in einen Place to be um. Schwarz und Weiß dominieren die Lobby. Dunkles Eichenparkett, beigefarbene Ledersessel, wengefarbene Möbel und Plisseeleuchten sind weitere Gestaltungselemente. Ein überdimensionierter Spiegel im Empfangsbereich findet sein Pendant in der Bristol Summerlounge, einem asiatisch inspirierten Garten mit Teichen, berankten Wänden und Holz-dielen. Die Hotelinhaber haben Frische in das alte Gemäuer gebracht: So etwa gibt es extravagante Beleuchtungs-Installationen hinter Vorhängen. Im Gang von der Lobby zu den Eventräumen wurden Wandkuben instal-liert, deren Dekoration sich je nach Jahreszeit oder Veranstaltung einem andern Thema widmet. Kosmopolitisch gibt sich auch die elegante Bristol Bar, die rund um die Uhr geöffnet ist.

01 | Dark oak parquet, black furniture and pleated lamps: the hotel lobby.

Dunkles Eichenparkett, schwarzes Mobiliar und Plisseelampen: die Hotellobby.

02 | Fresh and friendly colors can be found throughout the hotel. Flowers are arranged to match.

Frische und freundliche Farben finden sich im ganzen Hotel wieder. Blumen werden dazu passend arrangiert.

03 | The minimalist design concept of the public areas of the hotel is also carried through in the 145 rooms.

Auch in den 145 Zimmern setzt sich das minimalistische Designkonzept der öffentlichen Hotelbereiche fort.

03

cortiina | munich . germany
DESIGN: Albert Weinzierl

The name Cortiina divulges two preferences at once of its two owners—
their love of Italy and their enthusiasm for details that went into the design
of the 35-room hotel, with an eye to feng shui principles. Because eight
is the lucky number, an extra "i" was added to the name. People enter-
ing this hotel from the busy little Ledererstraße, with its whimsical, special
shops not far from the legendary Munich Hofbräuhaus, want to sit right
down in the lobby at the open fireplace, which is inset in a wall made of
natural Jurassic rock from the alpine upland. Guests will see a polished
version of that rock again in the bathroom. All materials used are as
natural as possible, and are given the chance to age beautifully through
use. The fine herringbone oak parquet remains unsealed, the leather
furniture was crafted with a special tanning procedure, and the high-
quality cotton sheets from Italy are unbleached. Most of the furniture was
designed especially for the hotel. A very special effect is created through
the folding wooden panels made of dark-stained bog oak which, when
opened, offer a view to the bathroom and lend the space a sense of gen-
erosity. Flat screens and wireless Internet access in all rooms contribute
to the comfort factor.

Am Namen des Cortiina lassen sich gleich zwei Vorlieben der beiden
Besitzer ablesen. Die Liebe zu Italien und die Detailversessenheit, mit
der das 35-Zimmer Hotel nach Feng Shui Kriterien gestaltet wurde. Weil
acht die entscheidende Glückszahl ist, wurde kurzerhand ein „i" addiert.
Wer das Hotel von der belebten kleinen Ledererstraße mit ihren witzigen,
besonderen Geschäften nicht weit vom legendären Münchner Hofbräuhaus betritt, möchte am liebsten gleich in der Lobby sitzen bleiben
am offenen Kamin, der eingelassen ist in eine Wand von geschichtetem
Naturstein-Jura aus dem Voralpenland. Dem Stein begegnet man dann
in geschliffener Form in den Badezimmern wieder. Alle verwendeten
Materialien sind möglichst naturbelassen und sollen die Chance haben,
durch den Gebrauch schön zu altern. Das edle Fischgrat-Eichenparkett
blieb unversiegelt, die Ledermöbel haben eine besondere Gerbung,
die hochwertige Baumwollbettwäsche aus Italien ist ungebleicht. Die
meisten Möbel wurden speziell für das Hotel entworfen. Ein sehr beson-
derer Effekt entsteht durch die faltbaren Holzfronten aus dunkel lasierter
Mooreiche, die aufgeklappt den Blick in die Badezimmer freigeben und
Großzügigkeit vermitteln. Flatscreens und Wireless-Internetzugang in allen
Räumen tragen zum Komfort bei.

01 | Glimpse from the bath into the room.

Blick vom Bad ins Zimmer.

02 | A mighty, wooden folding screen shields the fireplace area in the lobby.

Ein mächtiger hölzerner Paravent schirmt den Kaminbereich in der Lobby ab.

03 | The emphasis lies in extremely comfortable beds with rubber mattresses that offer heavenly slumber.

Der Fokus liegt auf äußerst bequemen Betten mit Kautschukmatratzen, in denen man himmlisch schläft.

03

hollmann beletage | vienna . austria

DESIGN: Christian Prasser

When a man with such an interesting professional history—cook, confectioner, actor—becomes a hotel owner, something exciting has got to result. In Vienna's refined, first district, a three-minute walk away from St. Stephan's Cathedral, Robert Hollmann operates a hotel, expanded to sixteen rooms, on the bel etage of a noble, Wilhelminian house: In his hotel, he can direct without limits, cook, and set the atmosphere of which he had always dreamt on his many trips. Of course, there is no hotel sign, and no lobby, but rather a salon with a blazing fireplace, where guests can read or converse, just as it always was in the fine houses of Vienna society. Because the hotel is surrounded by more than a millennium of history waiting to be discovered, the interior is reserved and contemporary. The most important design element is light, which seems to fall from the ceiling and run down along the walls, revealing the charm of the historical building structure and its uneven lines. In the rooms, the bathroom, television and wardrobe are hidden by a multifunctional wooden cabinet stretching across the entire length of the wall.

Wenn ein Mann mit einer so interessanten Berufsbiografie – Koch, Zuckerbäcker, Schauspieler – zum Hotelbesitzer wird, muss etwas Spannendes dabei herauskommen. Im feinen ersten Bezirk Wiens, drei Gehminuten vom Stephansdom entfernt, betreibt Robert Hollmann auf der Beletage eines noblen Gründerzeithauses ein auf sechzehn Zimmer erweitertes Hotel: In diesem kann er uneingeschränkt Regie führen, kochen und jene Atmosphäre inszenieren, von der er bei seinen vielen Reisen immer geträumt hat. Natürlich gibt es kein Hotelschild, keine Lobby, sondern einen Salon mit einem lodernden Kamin, wo man lesen oder ein Gespräch führen kann, genau so wie es ihn immer in den feinen Häusern der Wiener Gesellschaft gab. Weil es drum herum eine mehr als Jahrtausende alte Geschichte zu entdecken gilt, gibt sich das Interieur zurückhaltend und zeitgemäß. Wichtigstes Gestaltungselement ist das Licht, das von der Decke entlang den Wänden herunter zu fallen scheint und den Charme der Altbausubstanz durch deren Unebenheiten sichtbar macht. In den Zimmern verbergen sich hinter einer multifunktionalen Holzwand, die sich über die gesamte Längsseite zieht, Bad, Fernseher und Kleiderschrank.

02 | The modern rooms receive a Viennese flair through the old double windows and the herringbone parquet.

Wiener Flair erhalten die modern gestalteten Zimmer durch die alten Kastenfenster und das Fischgrätparkett.

02 03

02 | The modern rooms receive a Viennese flair through the old double windows and the herringbone parquet.

Wiener Flair erhalten die modern gestalteten Zimmer durch die alten Kastenfenster und das Fischgrätparkett.

03 | The bathroom is hidden behind a wall unit.

Das Badezimmer verbirgt sich hinter einer Schrankwand.

04 | With its small, two-person tables, long bench and vertical mirror, the breakfast room reflects the tradition of the classic Vienna coffee house.

Mit seinen kleinen Zweiertischen, der langen Bank und vertikalem Spiegel nimmt der Frühstücksraum die Tradition der klassischen Wiener Kaffeehäuser auf.

04

banys orientals | barcelona . spain

DESIGN: Lazaro Rosa

With the façade of an 18th century townhouse and its contemporary interior, this design hotel establishes remarkable contrasts between exterior and interior architecture. Clear lines, minimalist decoration, selected furniture and high-quality materials dominate the rooms. The philosophy of the house: Affordable, yet sophisticated. The idea is to bridge the gap between the expensive luxury hotels and the simple pensions. The 43 rooms and suites have especially wide and comfortable beds. Their design is similar to that of a canopy bed, but without the tacky curtains. There is a restaurant in the hotel that the locals also frequent for its national specialties. An oriental bath and sauna facility, which lent the Banys Orientals its name right from the start, is planned for the near future. Situated centrally in Barcelona's popular El Born district, it is just a few paces from the hotel to the Gothic quarter and the famous cathedral of St. Eulàlia.

Mit der Fassade eines im 18. Jahrhundert erbauten Stadthauses und seinem zeitgenössischen Interieurs setzt das Designhotel markante Kontraste zwischen Außen- und Innenarchitektur. Klare Linien, minimalistische Dekoration, ausgesuchte Möbel und hochwertige Materialien dominieren die Räumlichkeiten. Die Philosophie des Hauses: Bezahlbar, aber zugleich anspruchsvoll. Es soll damit die Lücke zwischen den teuren Luxushotels und den einfachen Pensionen geschlossen werden. Die 43 Zimmer und Suiten verfügen über besonders breite und komfortable Betten. Die Schlafgelegenheiten sind wie Himmelbetten konzipiert, auf kitschige Vorhänge wurde jedoch bewusst verzichtet. Im Hotel befindet sich ein Restaurant, das auch von Einheimischen, seiner landestypischen Spezialitäten wegen, gern besucht wird. Die Eröffnung einer orientalischen Bade- und Saunaanlage, die dem Banys Orientals schon von Beginn an seinen Namen gab, ist in naher Zukunft geplant. Zentral, im populären Bezirk El Born von Barcelona gelegen, sind es vom Hotel nur wenige Schritte zum Gotischen Viertel und der berühmten Kathedrale der heiligen Eulàlia.

01 | Lots of room to move: The beds have an especially wide design.

Viel Bewegungsfreiheit: Die Betten wurden besonders breit konzipiert.

02 | Among other dishes, the hotel restaurant serves Catalan
specialties.

Das Hotel Restaurant tischt unter anderem katalanische
Spezialitäten auf.

03 | Less is more: The decorative elements are minimalist, yet
exclusive.

Weniger ist mehr: Minimalistisch, aber exklusiv sind die
dekorativen Elemente.

04 | Clear lines define the concept of the hotel.

Eine klare Linienführung bestimmt das Konzept des Hauses.

05 | Behind a historical façade, the most modern of interior decorating
is revealed.

Hinter einer historischen Fassade verbirgt sich modernste
Innenausstattung.

de las letras hotel & restaurante | madrid . spain
DESIGN: Virgina Figueras

In a Wilhelminian-style building located on the Gran Via, the "hotel of literature" represents a successful synthesis of historical consciousness and modern design—not only in the selection of the furnishings and accessories, but also with regard to classical literature. The walls serve as display surfaces for literary quotations of famous writers and poets. The hotel's own library provides guests with the opportunity to relax with fine literature. The interior decoration, which exhibits its own, individual signature from floor to floor, is characterized by high, coffered ceilings, walls bearing typical Spanish tiles, or azulejos, stucco, and wrought-iron banisters. The countless style elements from the early 20th century stand in stimulating contrast to contemporary design.

In einem Gebäude aus der Gründerzeit an der Gran Via gelegen stellt das „Hotel der Literatur" eine gelungene Synthese aus Geschichtsbewusstsein und modernem Design dar. Nicht nur in der Auswahl des Mobiliars und der Accessoires, sondern auch in seinem Bezug zur klassischen Literatur. Die Wände dienen als Präsentationsfläche für literarische Zitate berühmter Schriftsteller und Dichter. Eine hauseigene Bibliothek gibt dem Gast Gelegenheit, sich bei anspruchsvoller Lektüre zu entspannen. Die Innenausstattung, von Stockwerk zu Stockwerk in individueller Handschrift, zeichnet sich durch hohe Räume mit Kassettendecken, Wände mit den typischen spanischen Fliesen, den Azulejos, Stuckarbeiten und schmiedeeisernem Geländer aus. Die unzähligen Stilelemente des frühen 20. Jahrhunderts treten auf spannungsreiche Weise mit dem Design der Gegenwart in Kontrast.

01 | Strong contrasts emphasize the sophisticated design.

Starke Kontraste unterstreichen das anspruchsvolle Design.

02 | On the sun deck above the roofs of Madrid.

Auf der Sonnenterrasse über den Dächern von Madrid.

03 | Beautiful views—thanks to room-high windows and doors.

Schöne Aussichten – raumhohe Fenster und Türen machen es
möglich.

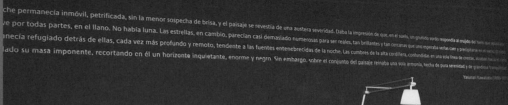

che permanecía inmóvil, petrificada, sin la menor sospecha de brisa, y el paisaje se revestía de una austera severidad. Daba la impresión de que, en el suelo, un gruñido sordo respondía al crujido del hielo que aplastaba ve por todas partes, en el llano. No había luna. Las estrellas, en cambio, parecían casi demasiado numerosas para ser reales, tan brillantes y tan cercanas que uno esperaba verlas caer y precipitarse en el suelo. El cielo necía refugiado detrás de ellas, cada vez más profundo y remoto, tendente a las fuentes entenebrecidas de la noche. Las cumbres de la alta cordillera, confundidas en una sola línea de crestas, alzaban hacia el cielo lado su masa imponente, recortando en él un horizonte inquietante, enorme y negro. Sin embargo, sobre el conjunto del paisaje reinaba una sola armonía, hecha de pura serenidad y de grandiosa tranquilidad.

Yasunari Kawabata (1899-1972)

04 | Each room is unique, and combines old and new in a distinctive manner.

Jedes Zimmer ist ein Unikat und verbindet Alt und Neu auf individuelle Weise.

05 | Quotations from famous writers and poets and its own library are the trademarks of this hotel.

Zitate berühmter Schriftsteller und Dichter und eine eigene Bibliothek sind das Markenzeichen des Hotels.

06 | A view into the lounge with its strong color accents.

Blick in die Lounge mit ihren starken Farbakzenten.

little palace hôtel | paris . france

DESIGN: Cabinet Interieur Design

Part of Paris' charm is imparted by its historical buildings. This is also true for the Little Palace Hôtel: Stonework, columns and wrought-iron balconies on the building's façade hail from the 19th century. Behind this old architecture, however, a contemporary atmosphere reveals itself to guests. In the open rooms, as in the 53 rooms and four suites of the hotel, large paintings by Viennese art nouveau artist Gustav Klimt set the tone. Their glittery world fits in seamlessly with the calm hand of the interior decorator. Light and dark woods lend a warm tone that is freshened up by the dabs of color provided by the dulcet green furniture and violet fabrics. Thus, the "city palace" generates a chic and at the same time romantic atmosphere. One of its highlights is most certainly the open view of the garden in the inner courtyard that can be enjoyed from the glass-roof restaurant as well as the intimacy of one's own balcony. Upon request, the hotel will also serve breakfast to you there. But then it's time to take to the streets, because the city with all of its sights and entertainment awaits. And the hotel's address is a perfect starting point.

Den Charme von Paris machen unter anderem seine historischen Bauwerke aus. Dergleichen gilt auch für das Little Palace Hôtel: Steinarbeiten, Säulen und schmiedeeiserne Balkone der Gebäudefront stammen noch aus dem vorletzten Jahrhundert. Hinter dieser alten Architektur öffnet sich den Logisgästen allerdings ein modern inspiriertes Ambiente. In den offenen Räumen wie in den 53 Zimmern und vier Suiten des Hotels geben großformatige Gemälde vom Wiener Jugendstilkünstler Gustav Klimt den Ton an. Dessen glitzernde Welt fügt sich nahtlos ein in die die ruhige Hand der Innenarchitektur. Hellere und dunklere Hölzer geben eine warme Tonalität vor, aufgefrischt von den Farbtupfern der lindgrünen Möbel und violetten Stoffe. So vermittelt der „Stadtpalast" eine schicke und gleichzeitig romantische Atmosphäre. Zu den Highlight gehört zweifellos der freie Blick auf den Garten im Innenhof, genießbar vom Glasüberdachten Restaurant wie in trauter Zweisamkeit vom Balkon der eigenen Bleibe aus. Dorthin serviert das Haus auf Wunsch auch das Frühstück. Dann aber heißt es hurtig, denn es wartet die Stadt mit all den vielen Sehenswürdigkeiten und Vergnügungen. Und dafür liegt die Adresse nachgerade ideal.

02

02 | 03 Regards from Klimt—a mixture of traditional substance and modern, colorful accents dictate the design of this antique hotel.

Klimt lässt grüßen - eine Mischung aus traditioneller Substanz und moderner, farbenfroher Akzente bestimmt das Design dieser alten Adresse.

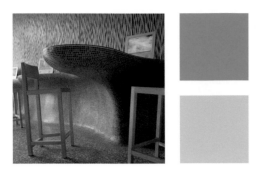

una hotel vittoria | florence . italy
DESIGN: Fabio Novembre

When globe trotters wake up in the morning, they cannot necessarily tell by the interchangeable look of many hotels in what country they are. You definitely will not find that phenomenon in Una Hotel Vittoria. The hotel, which opened in June of 2003, is a true Italian. Those expecting a design reflecting genteel reserve and a low-key atmosphere will be surprised. The hotel is bubbling with vitality, and, just as its fellow countrymen, is constantly telling new stories, starting with the noticeably floral design in the lobby, to the large seat sculptures in the bar to the giant historical wall paintings decorating the hallways. Italian designer Fabio Novembre is responsible for the firework of shapes and colors. In the design of the 84 rooms, he also focused on unusual lines and exciting lighting concepts. The goal was to make the house feel as lively and emotionally charged as possible. Despite the impressive variety, however, the decor is not gaudy. Thus, even guests seeking tranquility and solitude will find special corners in which to retreat. After all, one of the principles of Florentine hospitality is to respect visitors and fulfill all of their wishes.

Wenn ein Globetrotter morgens aufwacht, weiß er aufgrund der austauschbaren Optik vieler Hotels nicht unbedingt, in welchem Land er sich gerade befindet. Im Una Hotel Vittoria ist das mit Sicherheit anders. Das im Juni 2003 eröffnete Haus ist ein echter Italiener. Wer in Sachen Design vornehme Zurückhaltung und unaufdringliches Ambiente erwartet, ist hier falsch. Das Hotel sprüht vor Lebensfreude und erzählt wie seine Landsleute immer wieder neue Geschichten. Angefangen beim auffälligen floralen Design der Lobby, über großformatige Sitz-Skulpturen in der Bar bis hin zu den riesigen historischen Wandgemälden, die die Flure zieren. Für das Feuerwerk an Formen und Farben ist der italienische Designer Fabio Novembre verantwortlich. Er setzte auch bei der Gestaltung der insgesamt 84 Zimmer auf eine ungewöhnliche Linienführung und spannungsreiche Lichtkonzepte. Möglichst lebendig und emotionsgeladen sollte das Haus wirken. Trotz der beeindruckenden Vielfalt, ist die Einrichtung aber nicht laut. So findet auch der Gast, der Ruhe und Entspannung sucht, besondere Ecken in die er sich zurückziehen kann. Schließlich gehört es zu den Grundsätzen der florentinischen Gastfreundschaft, den Besucher zu respektieren und alle seine Wünsche zu erfüllen.

01 | The hotel forms a special contrast to the historical San Frediano district in which it is situated.

Das Hotel bildet einen besonderen Kontrast zum historischen Viertel San Frediano, in dem es liegt.

02 | Historical plus modern equals contemporary. In the hallways, Italian design epochs meet.

Historisch plus modern gleich zeitgemäß: In den Fluren treffen italienische Designepochen aufeinander.

03 | The extravagant cocktails served in the bar correspond to the decor.

Die extravaganten Cocktails, die in der Bar serviert werden, entsprechen der Einrichtung.

04 | Only gradually do visitors discover the many small design details waiting in every room.

Erst nach und nach entdecken Besucher die vielen kleinen Designdetails, die jedes Zimmer aufweist.

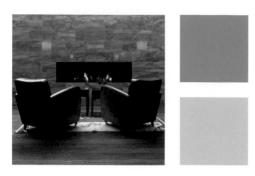

enterprise hotel | milan . italy

DESIGN: Sofia Gioia Vedani, Christina di Carlo, Christopher Redfern

The Enterprise Hotel is situated in a lively commercial district close to the former exhibition center, not too far away from the famous cathedral of Milan and the shopping streets of the Italian business, stock market, design and fashion capital. During the renovation of this former radio factory, the makers decided to preserve the industrial style of the building. This is clearly visible in the large windows of the restaurant and the high ceilings inside the building. The interior is impressive: Minimalist shapes were combined with classical and modern materials, such as stainless steel with shimmering, rainbow-colored tiles. Each detail was custom-made. The rooms, with their oriental antiques and discreet colors, generate a warm atmosphere. The 109 rooms and suites are equipped with designer furniture created exclusively for the hotel.

Das Enterprise Hotel liegt in einem lebendigen Geschäftsviertel in der Nähe des alten Messegeländes, nicht allzuweit entfernt vom berühmten Mailänder Dom und den Einkaufsstrassen der italienischen Business-, Börsen-, Design- und Modehauptstadt. Beim Umbau der ehemaligen Radiofabrik entschloss man sich den industriellen Stil des Gebäudes zu erhalten. Das zeigt sich deutlich an den großen Fenstern des Restaurants und den hohen Decken im Hausinneren. Das Interieur ist beeindruckend: Minimalistische Formen wurden mit klassischen und modernen Materialien kombiniert, zum Beispiel Edelstahl mit in Regenbogenfarben schillernden Fliesen. Jedes Detail wurde nach Maß verwirklicht. Die Räumlichkeiten schaffen mit ihren orientalischen Antiquitäten und den dezenten Farben eine warme Atmosphäre. Die 131 Zimmer und Suiten sind mit exklusiv für das Hotel entworfenen Designermöbeln ausgestattet.

02 | Wall paintings behind the shimmering mosaic of the sink area.

Wandgemälde hinter dem schillernden Mosaik des Waschblocks.

03 | High windows light up the function room.

Hohe Fenster erhellen den Veranstaltungs-Raum.

04 | Bedroom with parquet floor.

Schlafraum mit Parkettboden.

04

theoxenia | mykonos . greece

DESIGN: Angelos Angelopoulos, The Late Aris Constantinides, Yiannis Tsimas

Behind five old windmills on a small hill that seem to allegorically defy the winds of time, a total of 52 rooms and suites give an impression of the glamour of the Sixties. Simple furniture in the spirit of modern rationalism combines with the colorful sense of once-provocative pop art. Wing chairs, contoured seats, and vases are reminiscent of classics from such designers as Arne Jacobsen or Eero Saarinen. In the midst of all are floor lamps and sofas with decent flower patterns. This delight in the discreet charm of a retrospective design characterizes the hotel as a whole. It appears to be monolithic, where the blue and white tones are naturally a must. Even the bathrooms convey a taste for the bygone Sixties, completely decked out in those typical, small, colored tiles. The furnishings of the bathrooms in the rooms are certainly luxurious; the hotel sets high standards. With regard to these high standards, it is no surprise that a spa and a large, inviting pool are part of the picture.

Im Rücken von fünf alten Windmühlen, die auf einer kleinen Anhöhe scheinbar sinnbildlich dem Wind der Gezeiten trotzen, geben insgesamt 52 Zimmer und Suiten einen Eindruck vom Glamour der sechziger Jahre. Da mischt sich schlichtes Mobiliar im Geiste des modernen Rationalismus mit dem farbenfrohen Sinn der einst provokanten Popart. Ohrensessel, Schalensitze und Vasen erinnern an Klassiker etwa eines Arne Jacobsen oder Eero Saarinen. Mitten darin finden sich Stehlampen und Sofas mit dezentem Blumenmuster. Diese Freude am diskreten Charme eines retrospektiven Designs bestimmt das Hotel im Ganzen. Es erscheint wie aus einem Guss, bei dem der Farbklang von Blau und Weiß natürlich nicht fehlen darf. Selbst die Bäder vermitteln den Geschmack der verflossenen sechziger Jahre, durch und durch gefliest mit den so typischen kleinen Farbfliesen. Die Ausstattung der Zimmerbäder erweist sich als durchaus luxuriös, schließlich setzt das Hotel auf einen hohen Standard. Angesichts des hauseigenen Anspruchs verstehen sich ein Spa und ein einladend großer Pool von selbst.

02 | Like the hotel rooms, the pool has a modern elegance.

Genau wie in den Zimmern setzt man auch beim Pool auf
moderne Eleganz.

03 | 04 A few objects in the reception area supply the first allusions
to the cultivated style of the Sixties.

Einzelne Objekte beim Empfang weisen bereits auf den gepflegten
Stil der Sechziger Jahre hin.

05 | 06 | 07 Typical for a Greek holiday residence: the dominant blue and white tones.

Typisch für ein griechisches Feriendomizil: der dominante Farbklang von Blau und Weiß.

06

07

sumahan on the water | istanbul . turkey

DESIGN: Yasha Savcan Butler, Nedret Tayyibe Butler, Mark Horne Butler

The history of the building, which its owners, the architect pair the Butlers, transformed into a boutique hotel, stretches back to the year 1875: Where once raki was distilled, cosmopolitans wishing to discover Turkey now relax. With the exception of the bathrooms built with the marble typical of the country, the interiors provide a new interpretation to traditional Turkish culture elements and materials. Throughout the entire building, guests will find contemporary décor, most of which was designed by the daughter of the house, a young interior designer. As soon as guests arrive at the hotel, situated on the Asian side in the district of Cengelköy, they feel at home. In contrast to the hectic city, the atmosphere of the hotel has a calming effect, not lastly due to the unforgettable panorama of the Bosphorus that one has from every room and suite. Especially in the dark, the view is magnificent: Fishing boats, ferries and freighters glide past the windows; lights blink everywhere—a symbol for the lively metropolis. The surroundings of the chic and cosmopolitan hotel are characterized by traditional structures: Several houses are made of wood, there are promenades and fish restaurants—including the hotel's own award-winning fish and seafood restaurant, Kordon. During the 10-minute ride across the Bosphorus in the hotel boat to the European part of Istanbul, it is wise to keep your eyes open—to spot dolphins, which are a common sight here.

Bis in das Jahr 1875 reicht die Geschichte des Gebäudes zurück, das die Besitzer, das Architekten-Ehepaar Butler, zu einem Boutique-Hotel umgestaltet hat. Wo früher Raki gebrannt wurde, relaxen nun Kosmopoliten, die Istanbul entdecken wollen. Das Interieur ist, bis auf die im landestypischen Marmor gefertigten Badezimmer, eine neue Interpretation des türkischen Baustils. Im ganzen Haus findet sich zeitgenössische Einrichtung, die zum Großteil von der Tochter des Hauses, einer jungen Innenarchitektin, gestaltet wurde. Kommt man in dem auf der asiatischen Seite im Stadtteil Cengelköy gelegenem Hotel an, fühlt man sich sofort wie Zuhause. Im Kontrast zur hektischen Metropole wirkt die Atmosphäre des Hotels wie ein Pol der Ruhe: Nicht zuletzt wegen dem unvergleichlichen Blick auf den Bosporus, den man von allen Zimmern und Suiten aus hat. Besonders bei Dunkelheit ist dies ein Genuss: Fischerboote, Fähren und Frachter gleiten an den Fenstern vorbei; überall blinken Lichter – ein Sinnbild für die quirlige Metropole. Die Umgebung des schicken und kosmopolitischen Hotels ist geprägt von traditionellen Strukturen: Viele Häuser sind aus Holz gebaut, es gibt Promenaden und Fischlokale – so auch das hauseigene preisgekrönte Fisch- und Meeresfrüchte Restaurant Kordon. Bei der 10-minutigen Fahrt über den Bosporus mit dem hauseigenen Boot zum europäischen Teil Istanbuls, lohnt es sich die Augen offen zu halten – nach Delphinen, die hier keine Seltenheit sind.

01 | Suite with an open fire and a view of the Bosphorus.

Suite mit offenem Feuer und Bosporus-Blick.

02 | The hotel is situated in an old industrial building where the
waters of the Black and Marmara Seas mingle.

03 | Homage to the factory architecture: steel stairs and open masonry.

Hommage an die Fabrik-Architektur: Stahltreppe und offenes Mauerwerk.

04 | The loft suites on the ground floor have patio access.

Die Loftsuiten im Erdgeschoss haben Zugang zur Terrasse.

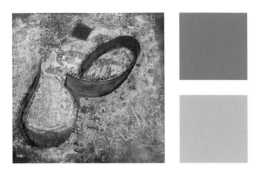

madada mogador | essaouira . morocco
DESIGN: Jonathan Amar

Small, but nice. With only five junior suites and one suite for up to four people, this hotel has a very clear layout. The first design hotel of the town is situated in the historical fortification of the port city of Essaouira and offers guests a direct view of the Atlantic. The interior combines modern design with traditional style. Thus, the bathrooms are adorned with exquisite Moroccan craftsmanship, from the ivory figures to the copper washbasins. The rooms are kept in soft colors—beige here, ochre there. All hotel guests have access to the spacious roof deck, which offers a panorama of the six-kilometer long beach. In addition, the beach, especially appreciated by windsurfers, as well as the harbor, can be directly accessed from the hotel. There, right on the water, freshly-caught fish is prepared before the eyes of diners in the outdoor restaurants.

Klein, aber fein. Mit nur fünf Junior-Suiten und einer Suite für bis zu vier Personen ist diese Herberge sehr übersichtlich gehalten. Das erste Designhotel des Ortes liegt in den historischen Befestigungsanlagen der Hafenstadt Essaouira und bietet seinen Gästen einen direkten Blick auf den Atlantik. Das Interieur verbindet modernes Design mit traditionellem Stil. So wurden die Bäder mit erlesener marokkanischer Handwerkskunst ausstaffiert, angefangen von Elfenbeinfiguren bis hin zum Kupferwaschbecken. Die Zimmer sind in sanften Farbtönen gehalten – mal in beige, mal in ockerrot. Alle Hotelgäste haben Zugang zu der weitläufigen Dachterrasse, von der sich ein Panorama-Blick auf den sechs Kilometer langen Strand bietet. Zu dem besonders von Windsurfern geschätzten Strand wie auch zum Hafen gibt es einen direkten Zugang vom Hotel. Dort, direkt am Wasser, wird frisch gefangener Fisch in Freiluft-Restaurants vor den Augen der Gäste zubereitet.

01 | View of the lounge, elegantly outfitted with designer furniture.

Blick in die mit Design-Möbeln elegant ausstaffierte Lounge.

02 | Soft colors dominate the look of the rooms.

Sanfte Farbtöne dominieren die Optik der Zimmer.

03 | Breakfast on the roof with a view of the Atlantic.

Frühstück auf der Terrasse – mit Blick auf den Atlantik.

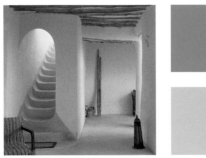

caravanserai | marrakesh . morocco

DESIGN: Mathieu Boccara, Max Lawrence

Centuries ago, Caravanserais were already offering accommodation to travelers along the significant trade routes in Northern Africa. There were places of rest and relaxation, but also places where traders could exchange important information. The name is composed of the words "caravan", travelers, and "sarai", home. The 17-room hotel in the Moroccan capital also strives to be a place of repose for travelers. Its architecture corresponds to the historical model: All rooms of the quadratic building are grouped around a central courtyard. Each room is reminiscent of stories from 1001 Arabian Nights. Wooden doors adorned with intricate ornamental metal fittings give way to views of a world of arched doorways and masoned cupolas. Hand-painted washbasins and woven bedspreads represent the traditional handicraft of the country. At dusk, hundreds of lanterns throughout the entire building create an especially romantic atmosphere. The traditional cuisine as well as the hotel's own hamam spa are dedicated to the physical well-being of the guests. In addition to the traditional steam bath, a variety of baths and massages with exotic oils are offered. Especially popular are the late-afternoon treatments, when guests return from an eventful day at the bazaars and museums of Marrakech.

Bereits vor Jahrhunderten boten Caravanserais Reisenden entlang der bedeutenden Handelsrouten in Nordafrika Unterkunft. Sie waren Ruhe- und Erholungsstätten, aber auch die Orte, an denen Händler wichtige Informationen austauschten. Der Name setzt sich aus den Worten „caravan" Reisende und „sarai" Heim zusammen. Auch das 17 Zimmer umfassende Haus in der marokkanischen Hauptstadt möchte Ruhepol für Reisende sein. Die Architektur entspricht dem historischen Vorbild: Alle Räume des viereckigen Gebäudes gruppieren sich um einen zentralen Innenhof. Jedes Zimmer erinnert an Geschichten aus Tausendundeiner Nacht. Mit aufwändigen Ornamenten beschlagene Holztüren öffnen Einblick in eine Welt geschwungener Türbogen und gemauerter Deckenkuppeln. Handbemalte Waschbecken und gewebte Tagesdecken repräsentieren die traditionelle Handwerkskunst des Landes. Für eine besonders romantische Atmosphäre sorgen nach Einbruch der Dunkelheit hunderte von Laternen im ganzen Gebäude. Dem körperlichen Wohl widmet sich die traditionelle Küche genauso wie das hauseigene Hamam. Neben dem traditionellen Dampfbad werden verschiedene Bäder und Massagen mit exotischen Ölen angeboten. Besonders begehrt sind die Anwendungen am späten Nachmittag, wenn die Gäste von einem erlebnisreichen Tag auf den Basaren und in den Museen Marrakeschs zurückkehren.

01 | Sleep comes like a fairy-tale—thanks to the architecture, it stays pleasantly cool, even in summer.

Schlafen wie im Märchen – dank der Bauweise auch im Sommer angenehm kühl.

02 | Most of the action takes place in the courtyard, which the restaurant with the open hearth borders.

Ein Großteil des Lebens spielt sich im Innenhof ab, an den auch das Restaurant mit offenem Feuer grenzt.

03 | Where in former times traders lodged their animals, today guests find generous common rooms.

Wo in vergangenen Zeiten Händler ihre Tiere unterbrachten, findet der Gast heute großzügige Aufenthaltsräume.

jardin d'ébène | cape town . south africa

DESIGN: Pascale Lauber & Ulrike Bauschke

Jardin D'ébène presents itself as a Victorian villa on the hills of Cape Town. The small but inviting guesthouse—opened in 2003—is a true insider tip for anyone looking for something unique. With their ten years of gastronomic experience and their passion for interior decorating, the two owners, Ulrike and Pascale, have created an unmistakable flair. Each of the four guest rooms has its own style, furnished according to the animals zebra, elephant, lion and cheetah. The rooms are grouped around the living room that opens to the garden. At breakfast or an evening glass of wine outdoors, among banana trees, wooden sculptures, a sun deck and miniature pool, an atmosphere reminiscent of an urban bush camp arises right in the heart of Cape Town. The owners place great value on making sure that the spirit of optimism, creativity and positive energy prevailing in South Africa will also rub off on the hotel's guests.

Jardin D'ébène präsentiert sich als viktorianische Villa am Hang von Kapstadt. Das kleine, aber feine Gästehaus – 2003 eröffnet – ist ein echter Geheimtipp für jeden, der das Individuelle sucht. Mit der zehnjährigen gastronomischen Erfahrung der beiden Inhaberinnen Ulrike und Pascale und ihrer Leidenschaft für Innenarchitektur haben sie ein unverwechselbares Flair geschaffen. Jedes der vier Gästezimmer hat seinen eigenen Stil, eingerichtet nach den Tieren Zebra, Elefant, Löwe und Schimpanse. Die Räume gruppieren sich um den zum Garten hin offenen Wohnraum. Beim Frühstück oder dem abendlichen Wein im Freien kommt zwischen Bananenstauden, Holzskulpturen, Sonnendeck und Minipool mitten in Kapstadt das Ambiente eines urbanen Buschcamps auf. Den Inhaberinnen ist sehr wichtig, dass die in Südafrika herrschende Aufbruchstimmung, Kreativität und positive Energie auch von den Gästen des Hotels aufgegriffen wird.

01 | A place of inspiration: Garden with chaise lounges and tropical plants.

Ort der Inspiration: Garten mit Liegen und tropischen Gewächsen.

02 03

02 | A view of one of the guest rooms.

Blick in eins der Gästezimmer.

03 | Open living room with an African interior.

Offener Wohnraum mit afrikanischem Interieur.

01 | The modern kitchen of Melbourne chef Teage Ezard follows the design concept.

Die moderne Küche des Melbourner Chefkochs Teage Ezard folgt dem Designkonzept.

jia hongkong | hong kong . hong kong

DESIGN: Philippe Starck

Outside, life is noisy. There is beeping, ringing, hammering, and talking. Home to millions, the city of Hong Kong challenges its visitors; it captivates all of the senses. Almost seven million people are crowed into an area not much larger than metropolitan Frankfurt. Here, the former British colony unites tradition and modernity in a unique way. It is hard to imagine that Hong Kong was a small fishing community on the southern tip of China right up into the 19th century. Its development into a trade metropolis occurred very rapidly. Even today, traces of Hong Kong's changing history can be discovered everywhere in the city. Especially in the Causeway Bay area of Hong Kong Island, you can find giant department stores just as easily as traditional Chinese markets. It is incredibly difficult to escape the magnetism of this city, and yet quite easy. It is just a few steps from the hectic pace of Chinese life to the tranquillity of the JIA Boutique Hotel, opened in 2004. Jia is Mandarin, and means home. And that is exactly what JIA strives to be: A home far away from home. The hotel was the first in all of Asia to be designed by Philippe Starck. The design guru had exactly 24 floors and 57 suites to implement his ideas. The result is the perfect symbiosis between Asia and Europe. Exclusive service is a natural part of the hotel concept, which, by the way, at JIA also means giving guests the opportunity to do their own laundry, just like at home.

Draußen lärmt das Leben. Es hupt, klingelt, hämmert, redet. Die Millionenmetropole Hong Kong fordert ihre Besucher, sie fesselt alle Sinne. Auf einer Fläche, die nicht viel größer ist als der Großraum Frankfurt, drängen sich fast sieben Millionen Menschen. Dabei vereint die ehemalige britische Kolonie Tradition und Moderne auf besondere Art und Weise. Kaum vorstellbar, dass Hong Kong bis ins 19. Jahrhundert eine kleine Fischergemeinde am Südzipfel Chinas war. Die Entwicklung zur Handelsmetropole verlief umso rasanter. Noch heute lassen sich Spuren Hong Kongs wechselvoller Geschichte überall in der Stadt entdecken. Besonders im Viertel Causeway Bay auf Hong Kong Island findet man riesige Warenhäuser genauso wie traditionelle chinesische Märkte. Dem Sog dieser Stadt zu entkommen, ist unendlich schwer und doch ganz leicht. Nur ein paar Schritte sind es von der Hektik des chinesischen Lebens in die Ruhe des 2004 eröffneten JIA Boutique Hotels. Jia ist Mandarin und bedeutet Heimat. Und genau das will das JIA sein: Eine Heimat weit weg von der Heimat. Das Hotel wurde, als erstes in ganz Asien, von Philippe Starck designt. Genau 24 Stockwerke und 57 Suiten hatte der Designguru, um seine Vorstellungen umzusetzen. Das Ergebnis ist die perfekte Synthese von Asien und Europa. Exklusiver Service gehört selbstverständlich zum Hotelkonzept, darunter versteht man im JIA übrigens auch, den Gästen die Möglichkeit zu geben, ganz wie zu Hause, die eigene Wäsche selbst zu waschen.

03 | 04

05

02 | Every room includes ultra-modern technical equipment and
a swivelling flat-screen television.

Zu jedem Zimmer gehört eine ultra-moderne technische
Ausstattung mit drehbarem Flachbildfernseher.

03 | Philippe Starck combines Asian room concepts with European
furniture.

Asiatische Raumkonzepte kombiniert Philippe Starck mit
europäischem Mobiliar.

04 | All guests can cook for themselves in the fully-equipped kitchens
in each room.

Jeder Gast kann in der voll ausgestatteten Küche seines Zimmers
selbst kochen.

05 | The studios in JIA measure 380 square metres; the two penthouse
suites amount to 1570 square metres.

Die Studios im JIA sind 380 Quadratmeter groß, die zwei
Penthouse-Suiten umfassen 1570 Quadratmeter.

01 | A view from the hotel's roof deck reveals the lack of space in the
former British Crown Colony.

Ein Blick von der Dachterrasse des Hotels zeigt den Platzmangel
in der ehemaligen britischen Kronkolonie.

m hotel singapore | singapore . singapore

DESIGN: Kanko Kikaku Sekkeisha, Isabelle Miaja & Associates, Zuria Design

In a city calling one of the most modern and largest ports of the world its own, in which the focus is on finance, economy and commerce, work, of course, is a virtue. So naturally the owners of the m hotel are proud of the many awards that it has garnered as the best medium-sized business hotel in Asia. The decor corresponds to the adage that "form follows function". Each of the 413 rooms has a generously-sized work area, equipped with the latest technology. The hotel's four restaurants and bars ensure that a stay here can not only be productive but also relaxing. The cuisine is one of the few distinctly Asian elements, as the room furnishings, the conference rooms and lobby are oriented toward Western standards. This means that there are neither typically Asian patterns nor furniture. Steel and glass, in combination with wood and European design classics ensure an emphatically unobtrusive atmosphere. These furnishings are intended to form a clear contrast to the pulsing metropolis of Singapore. After all, with the numerous impressions of this giant city, which covers a majority of the island nation, it is often difficult to concentrate on the essentials.

In einer Stadt, die einen der modernsten und größten Häfen der Welt ihr eigen nennt, in der sich alles um Finanzen, Wirtschaft und Handel dreht, ist Arbeit selbstverständlich eine Tugend. So ist man im M Hotel stolz auf die diversen Auszeichnungen, die das Haus als bestes Mittelklasse Business Hotel Asiens gewonnen hat. Die Einrichtung entspricht dem Grundsatz „form follows function". Jedes der 413 Zimmer hat einen großzügig geschnittenen Arbeitsbereich, ausgestattet mit der neuesten Technik. Dafür, dass der Aufenthalt der Gäste nicht nur produktiv, sondern auch erholsam ist, sorgen die vier hauseigenen Restaurants und Bars. Die Küche gehört zu den wenigen eindeutig asiatischen Elementen, denn die Möblierung der Zimmer, der Konferenzräume und der Lobby orientiert sich an westlichen Standards. Das heißt, es gibt weder typisch asiatische Muster noch Möbel. Stahl und Glas sorgen in Verbindung mit Holz und europäischen Designklassikern für ein betont unaufdringliches Ambiente. Mit dieser Einrichtung will man bewusst einen klaren Kontrast zur pulsierenden Metropole Singapur schaffen. Schließlich fällt es bei der Vielzahl der Eindrücke dieser riesigen Stadt, die einen Großteil des Inselstaats einnimmt, oft nicht leicht, sich auf das Wesentliche zu konzentrieren.

03 04

05

02 | On the 29 floors, there are only a few spots that are Asian-inspired.

In den 29 Stockwerken gibt es nur wenige Ecken, die asiatisch inspiriert sind.

03 | From their rooms, guests either look onto the impressive skyline or the sea.

Von seinem Zimmer blickt der Gast entweder auf die beeindruckende Skyline oder aufs Meer.

04 | Numerous conference rooms and communication-friendly lounges emphasize the hotel's business consciousness.

Zahlreiche Konferenzräume und kommunikativ gestaltete Lounges unterstreichen den Business-Anspruch des Hauses.

05 | "We don't give you anything that you don't need", says the Management regarding the design concept.

„Wir geben Ihnen nichts, was Sie nicht brauchen", so beschreibt das Management das Designkonzept.

06 | In the comfortable room temperatures, guests hardly notice the
tropical, humid climate.

Vom tropisch schwülen Klima bekommt der Gast in den
angenehm temperierten Räumen kaum etwas mit.

united hotel | taipei . taiwan
DESIGN: Lu Shi-Chieh

Minimalist design, timeless elegance and flattering natural tones. That is how stylish the first design hotel of Taiwan looks. The United Hotel is situated in the heart of the bustling commercial city of Taipei, surrounded by the most important shopping centers and within walking distance to Taipei World Trade Center. Due to its central location, it is one of the top addresses for business travelers. Nevertheless, it has nothing in common with the uniform business hotels, but rather, it was able to preserve the charm of a modestly-sized house with a great deal of personal atmosphere and tranquility. Taiwan-based architect Lu Shi-Chieh took a discreet color palette and natural materials to create a modern interpretation of oriental architecture mixed with western influences. The rooms are functionally furnished, with extra-large built-in closets, chocolate-colored couches, beds with thick, starched linens and cherry wood desks. White walls and gray carpets supply a balanced contrast to the dark colors of the furniture. In almost every room, large windows extending to the floor open out to fascinating perspectives of the city skyline.

Minimalistisches Design, zeitlose Eleganz und schmeichelnde Naturtöne. So stilvoll präsentiert sich das erste Designhotel Taiwans. Das United Hotel liegt im Herzen der wirtschaftlich quirligen Metropole Taipeh, umgeben von den wichtigsten Shoppingzentren und in Gehweite vom Taipeh World Trade Center. Durch seine zentrale Lage zählt es zur ersten Adresse für Geschäftsreisende. Trotzdem hat es nichts mit den uniformen Businesshotels gemein, sondern hat sich den Charme eines überschaubaren Hauses mit viel persönlicher Atmosphäre und Ruhe bewahren können. Der in Taiwan ansässige Architekt Lu Shi-Chieh hat mit dezenter Farbwahl und natürlichen Materialien eine moderne Interpretation fernöstlicher Architektur gemischt mit westlichen Einflüssen geschaffen. Die Zimmer sind funktionell ausgestattet, mit übergroßen Einbauschränken, schokoladenfarbigen Couchs, Betten mit dicken, gestärkten Leinenbezügen sowie Kirschbaumholz-Schreibtischen. Weiße Wände und graue Teppichböden bieten einen ausgewogenen Kontrast zu den dunklen Farbtönen des Mobiliars. Durch große Fenster, die bis zum Boden reichen, eröffnen sich aus fast jedem Zimmer faszinierende Perspektiven auf die Skyline der Metropole.

02 | Simple yet elegant rooms with whimsical glass windows to the
bathroom.

Schlichte aber elegante Zimmer mit neckischen Glasfenstern
zum Bad hin.

02

03 | Tranquil oasis amid the commercial city of Taipei.

Ruhige Oase inmitten der Wirtschaftsmetropole Taipeh.

the prince | melbourne . australia
DESIGN: Allan Powell, Paul Hecker

Actually, The Prince does not deserve its name. According to several regular guests, the hotel, opened in 1999, has long since earned the king's throne among the boutique hotels in the Australian state of Victoria. Not only the 40-room hotel itself, but also the hotel's own Aurora Spa Retreat, the award-winning Restaurant Circa and the exclusive Wodka bar Mink are well-known far beyond the borders of Melbourne. Every separate area was individually designed. The lobby was designed with a purposefully theatrical look; the sun-drenched roof deck exhibits Moroccan elements, and guests can enjoy a Mediterranean flair when dining under olive trees in the courtyard. The individual rooms also have no trace of typical Australian clichés. Instead of paintings of red earth and kangaroos, guests will find design classics and light colors. In addition to the extraordinary design, there is another aspect of the hotel that makes it so popular—the uncomplicated, open manner of the Australians. If you are lucky, you might meet a boat owner at the bar who will casually invite you to take a sail the next day. That is, after all, the best way to discover the picturesque Port Phillip Bay, situated just a few meters from the hotel, with its marina and breathtaking view of the Melbourne skyline.

Seinen Namen hat The Prince eigentlich nicht verdient. Längst hat das 1999 eröffnete Haus, nach Aussagen zahlreicher Stammgäste, den Königsthron unter den Boutique Hotels im australischen Bundesstaat Victoria inne. So ist nicht nur das 40 Zimmer umfassende Hotel selbst, sondern auch das hauseigene Aurora Spa Retreat, das preisgekrönte Restaurant Circa und die exklusive Wodka-Bar Mink weit über die Grenzen Melbournes hinaus bekannt. Jeder einzelne Bereich wurde individuell gestaltet. Ganz bewusst theatralisch ist die Lobby eingerichtet. Sonnendurchflutet mit marokkanischen Elementen zeigt sich die Dachterrasse und mediterranen Flair genießt, wer im Innenhof unter Olivenbäumen diniert. Die einzelnen Zimmer haben ebenfalls nichts mit den typischen Australien-Klischees gemein. Statt Gemälde von roter Erde und Kängurus findet man hier Designklassiker und helle Farben. Neben dem außergewöhnlichen Design, macht vor allem ein Aspekt das Boutique Hotel so beliebt – der unkomplizierte, weltoffene Stil der Australier. Wer Glück hat, lernt an der Bar einen Bootsbesitzer kennen, der für den nächsten Tag ganz unverbindlich zu einer Segeltour einlädt. Schließlich ist das der beste Weg, die nur ein paar hundert Meter vom Hotel entfernte malerische Port Phillip Bay mit ihrem Yachthafen und dem atemberaubenden Blick auf die Melbourner Skyline zu erkunden.

01 | Soft materials and mellow colors contribute to the consciously calming atmosphere of the rooms.

Softe Materialen und sanfte Farben tragen zur bewusst beruhigenden Atmosphäre der Zimmer bei.

02 | The artist Mike Parr painted a few pictures just for The Prince.

Der Künstlers Mike Parr hat einige Gemälde extra für The Prince angefertigt.

03

03 | The hotel's own Aurora Spa Retreat is one of the largest and best in all of Australia.

Das hauseigene Aurora Spa Retreat gehört zu den größten und besten in ganz Australien.

hotel adagio | san francisco . california
DESIGN: Colum McCartan

San Francisco is such a Victorian city that it is easy to forget an architectural influence that predominates in other areas of California, Spanish Colonial Revival. The Adagio is a wonderful example of that style with its lace-like façade, its Moorish window shapes and ornate balconies. The interior continues this theme but in a modern and fresh way. The lobby and the reception area are more modern Spanish and in keeping with the restaurant of the hotel, the brightly decorated Cortez, named after the Spanish explorer Hernando Cortez. Only the unusual shape of the large lobby windows reminds the visitor of the traditional façade. The guest rooms have modern lines but the colors and materials repeat the Spanish colonial feel. More neutral beiges and browns are offset by dark rust, strong olive green and dusty blue. The dark stained wood furniture pieces with their clean lines also match this delicate balance between traditional and modern. Even the washstands are dark stained wood and have a rustic appeal with a very modern esthetic. Modern artwork and mirrors with solid wood frames complete the look.

San Francisco ist eine so viktorianische Stadt, dass man leicht vergisst, dass der vorherrschende Baustil Kaliforniens der spanische Kolonialstil ist. Das Adagio Hotel ist ein schönes Beispiel für diesen Stil, mit seiner spitzenartigen Fassade, den maurisch anmutenden Fenstern und den verzierten Balkonen. Die Lobby und die Lounge des Hotels sind eher in zeitgenössisch spanischem Stil eingerichtet so wie auch das Hotelrestaurant Cortez, das nach dem Spanischen Entdecker Hernando Cortez benannt ist. Nur die ungewöhnliche Form der Fenster erinnert den Besucher an das traditionelle Äußere des Hotels. Die Schlafzimmer sind modern eingerichtet aber die Farbgebung orientiert sich am spanischen Kolonialstil. Neutrale Erdtöne werden von dunklen Rottönen, Olive und Graublau ergänzt. Die dunkel gebeizten aber geradlinigen Möbel sind auch Teil dieser Gratwanderung zwischen traditionell und modern. Sogar die Waschstände aus dunklem Holz reflektieren das Thema. Zeitgenössische Kunst und Spiegel in dunklen Holzrahmen vervollständigen das Designkonzept bis ins kleinste Detail.

01 | Bedroom color scheme.

Schlafzimmerfarben.

02 | Lobby with Moorish windows.

Die Lobby mit ihren maurischen Fenstern.

03 04

03 | The Bolero Penthouse on the 16th floor expresses an urban loft-style with its fireplace.

Das Bolero Penthouse auf der 16. Etage repräsentiert mit seinem offenen Kamin den urbanen Loft-Stil.

04 | The minimalist ornaments reflect a fresh design that bridges its Spanish Colonial Revival.

Die minimalistischen Ornamente entsprechen einem erfrischenden Design, das den spanischen Kolonialstil wiederaufleben lässt.

05 | The bathroom also has a clean and contemporary design aesthetic.

Auch im Badezimmer eine klare und zeitgenössische Formsprache.

the mosser | san francisco . california
DESIGN: Your Space

The Mosser was built in 1913. It is a beautiful Victorian hotel that was considered one of the cities most luxurious at that time. A change in ownership and a renovation gave it a more contemporary feel. The shell of the building and everything that was attached to the building itself was carefully restored: the marble floors and the ornately decorated ceilings, the bay windows and the stained glass accents. At the same time, the furniture and the art have a more contemporary feel. Every room has a combination of the old and the new. The traditional lobby is decorated with a large patent leather couch and with brightly colored pillows. The beautiful bay windows in the guest rooms have traditional window seats but next to them a modern platform bed. The predominant colors are white walls and brown fabrics to complement the darkly stained wood, with bright accent colors. The theme of natural colors and materials reflects the environmental involvement of the owners. A percentage of the profits are donated to reforestation projects and organically grown apples are available everywhere in the hotel.

Das Mosser Hotel wurde 1913 gebaut. Das viktorianische Gebäude galt damals als eines der der luxuriösesten der Stadt. Ein neuer Besitzer und eine Renovierung haben es von Grund auf modernisiert. Das Gebäude selbst und alle existierenden Anbauten wurden behutsam erneuert. Akzente setzen die Marmorböden, Stuckdecken, Erkerfenster und farbigen Glastüren. Gleichzeitig sind die neuen Möbel und Accessoires modern. Jedes Zimmer ist eine Kombination von Alt und Neu. Die traditionelle Lobby ist mit einer Lackledercouch und farbigen Stoffen ausgestaltet. Die modernen Plattformbetten der Schlafzimmer stehen neben den eingebauten Erkerbänken. Die vorherrschende Farbgebung sind weiße Wände, braune Stoffe die zu dem dunklen Parkett und den hellen klaren Farben passen. Die natürlichen Farben und Materialien spiegeln das Umweltbewusstsein des Besitzers wider, der einen Teil des Profits für das Bepflanzen von neuen Wäldern spendet. Bio-Äpfel sind im ganzen Hotel in großen Schalen verteilt zu finden.

01 | Typical bedroom with bay window.
Typisches Erkerfenster und Bett.

02 | Lobby with patent leather seat.

   Lobby mit Lackcouch.

03 | Suite.

   Suite.

03

élan hotel modern | los angeles . california

DESIGN: Trevor Abramson, Melanie Rechnitz

The architect's challenge: how to turn a former convalescent home into a stylish hotel on a tight budget. The exterior had an interesting canopy structure over the roof, a big sign and a tiled front façade. The architect added canopies over the entrance, had the exterior limestone tiles painted a bright blue and opened the whole front of the lobby to the street. Beverly Boulevard has a high concentration of furniture stores, many of them mid-century antiques. By giving the lobby large storefront windows, the lobby design and the visitors in it become the main focal point of the hotel. The lobby colors: aqua, ochre and lime green are set against a concrete floor and the mahogany reception desk. The mood is at the same time glamorous and cool. The late 60's appeal of the existing structure showcases the new design accents that were woven into it. This is a very subtle renovation where the designer decided to strengthen the features that were there instead of erasing them. The rooms are decorated in soothing neutral earth tones. Black and white photographs of nature close-ups add to the theme of the hotel where the line between old and new is not always clear.

Dic Herausforderung des Architekten war es, mit einem sehr begrenzten Budget eine ehemalige Rehaklinik in ein modernes Hotel umzubauen. Das Äußere des Gebäudes zeigt ein baldachinartiges Dach, ein großes Schild und eine gekachelte Außenfassade. Der Architekt entwarf ein Vordach um den Eingang zu markieren, ließ die Kacheln blau streichen und öffnete den Grossteil der Fassade zur Strasse hin. Auf dem Beverly Boulevard – wo sich das Hotel befindet – reiht sich ein Möbelgeschäft ans andere, viele von ihnen mit 50er und 60er Jahre Antiquitäten. Indem die Lobby wie ein großes Schaufenster aussieht, werden die Einrichtung und ihre Besucher zur Ausstellungsware. Die Farben der Lobby, Aqua, Ocker und Limonengrün stehen im Kontrast zu dem neutralen Betonboden und der Mahagoni-Rezeption. Die Atmosphäre ist glamourös und gleichzeitig cool. Die 60er Jahre Ästhetik des Baus ist ein guter Hintergrund für die neuen Elemente die eingewoben wurden. Es ist eine sehr behutsame Form der Renovierung. Die vorhandenen gestalterischen Elemente sollten verstärkt statt versteckt werden. Die Hotelzimmer sind in neutralen Erdtönen gehalten. Schwarz-Weiß-Aufnahmen von Pflanzen spiegeln das Thema des Hotels, mit der nicht immer klar definierten Trennlinie zwischen Alt und Neu wider.

01 | View from lobby.

Blick von der Lobby.

02

03

the farmer's daughter | los angeles . california

DESIGN: Dean Larkin Design, delta Wright-Interior Design

Directly across from the Farmer's Market, this motel from the 60's needed a remodel. A recent renovation completely changed the look but kept the name. Not only did they keep the name but they made it into the theme: a psychedelic mix of farm tools and pop-art colors. The colors of the exterior and the lobby are different shades of turquoise and ochre. The chunky stained wood furniture and reception desk add a rustic feel. Oversized farm tools are hung on the exterior courtyard walls and brightly printed pillows are strewn around on the courtyard furniture. The surprise comes in the late afternoon. The strong colors of the courtyards soften and glow in the golden pink light of a typical Californian sunset and reflect the sky and the twinkling lights of the city around it. The rooms all have a farm theme as well, with gingham prints and denim bedspreads. The ironic accents that make this bearable in the public spaces are missing here. But, with a pool and a beautiful courtyard, who would spend a lot of time in their rooms?

Direkt gegenüber vom Farmers Market lag ein 60er Jahre Motel, das es dringend galt zu renovieren. Es wurde modernisiert, der Name aber beibehalten. Nicht nur das, er wurde zum Entwurfs-Thema: ein subversiver Mix aus Bauernhof und Popfarben. Die Außenfassade und Lobby sind in verschiedenen Türkis- und Ockertönen gehalten. Große Harken und Schaufeln hängen an den Wänden der Innenhöfe und bunte Sitzkissen sind auf den rustikalen Gartenmöbeln verteilt. Abends verändert sich die Atmosphäre. Die starken Farben fangen im rosa Licht des kalifornischen Sonnenuntergangs an zu leuchten und eins zu werden mit dem Himmel und den aufflackernden Lichtern der Stadt. Die Schlafzimmer haben das gleiche Bauernhofthema der Lobby, mit karierten Kissen und Jeansdecken. Nur fehlt hier etwas die Ironie die das Thema in den öffentlichen Räumen erträglich macht. Aber, wer wird schon viel Zeit in seinem Zimmer verbringen, wenn der Innenhof und der Pool warten?

01 | Smaller courtyard with pool.

Kleiner Hof mit Schwimmbad.

02 | Lobby and larger courtyard.

Lobby und großer Innenhof.

clinton south beach | miami . florida

D E S I G N : Eric Raffy

From the outside, the hotel looks like a typical art deco South Beach Hotel. Right in the middle of the liveliest stretch of South Beach, near the ocean, architect Eric Raffy has re-designed the interiors and courtyards to achieve a level of calm and relaxation. The interior colors correspond to the palette you will see outside: blues, greens and grays, but the designs are a cleaner, more modern interpretation of the curved shapes and horizontal lines of the art deco style. Stylistically, the lobby is the transition point from the traditional exterior and the modern interior. The reception desk and the lounge furniture are reminiscent of the 30's but at the same time edgier with bondage and corset details. Once you step into the courtyard, you will be in a fresher and more contemporary environment. A long narrow lap pool defines the outdoor space and also acts as a canal for the rooms just above it. Balconies, designed like pool cabanas, overlook it and give it a beach-like atmosphere. The rooms have the same fresh beach feel with a reduced white, gray and sage color theme. Open sink and bath areas continue the water theme of the outside and give the rooms a cooling spa feel.

Von außen sieht das Hotel aus wie ein typisches South Beach Hotel im Art déco Stil. Im Innern hat der Architekt Eric Raffy eine entspannende und ruhige Atmosphäre geschaffen. Die Farben des Interieurs verschwimmen mit denen, die man am South Beach sieht: Blau, Grün und Grau. Die Formgebung ist eine klarere, modernere Interpretation der Kurven und der horizontalen Betonung des Art déco Stils. Die Lobby ist eine Mischung aus traditioneller Fassade und moderner Innenraumgestaltung. Die Rezeption und die Lounge erinnern an die 30er Jahre, sind aber gleichzeitig gewagter durch Fessel-und-Korsett Details. Sobald man den Innenhof betritt, ist man in einer frischeren Umgebung: Ein langes Schwimmbecken definiert den Außenraum und fungiert als Kanal für die Zimmer mit direktem Blick darauf. Balkone die wie Strandkörbe aussehen geben dem Ganzen eine Ferienstimmung. Die Schlafzimmer haben das gleiche frische Strandgefühl mit den reduzierten Farben Weiß, Grau und Salbeigrün. Ein offener Badebereich wiederholt das Wasserthema der Innenhöfe und gibt den Zimmern eine kühlende Spa-Atmosphäre.

01 | Cabana balconies overlooking the pool.
Strandkorb-Balkone über dem Pool.

02 | View from open bath into bedroom.
   Blick vom offenen Bad in den Schlafbereich.

03 | Exterior art deco façade.
   Art déco Fassade.

04 | Lobby and reception area.
   Lobby und Lounge.

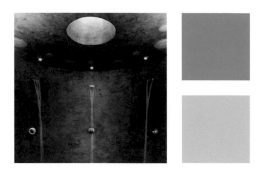

the standard miami | miami . florida
DESIGN: André Balazs

It must be hard to be André Balazs. With every new hotel everybody is curious to see how he has "raised the standard" again. The new Standard Hotel in Miami is going to exceed any expectations. The old Lido Spa Hotel has been revamped into a quiet, exclusive and completely over-the-top spa. The marble walls and terrazzo floors where kept, as well as the stainless steel elevators. What was added was a secondary layer of Scandinavian spa theme. The strong primary colors of a Swedish summer house were added as well as the slatted wood walls of a Finnish sauna. The spa is concentrating on all forms of water treatments, most of them in public places. The outdoor bathing area features a hot tub, plunging pool and a falling water column. A Turkish style hamam, a Swedish sauna and an infinity pool are all designed as a communal experience. The hotel is located on Belle Isle, away from the party scene of Miami.

Es ist bestimmt nicht einfach André Balazs zu sein. Mit jedem seiner neuen Hotels ist man von allen Seiten gespannt, wie er diesmal den „Standard" neu definiert. Das neue Standard in Miami wird jede Erwartung übertreffen. Das ehemalige Lido Spa Hotel ist in einen ruhigen, exklusiven, komplett Superlativ-Spa umgebaut worden. Die Marmorwände, Terrazzo-Böden und Stahlaufzüge wurden erhalten. Wie eine zweite Entwurfsebene wurde dem Design ein skandinavisches Sauna-Thema hinzugefügt. Dass die beiden Ebenen nicht unbedingt zusammen passen, macht den Reiz aus. Die kräftigen Primärfarben eines schwedischen Sommerhauses sind überall zu finden, ebenso wie die typischen Holzlattenverschalungen einer finnischen Sauna. Das Spa konzentriert sich auf alle Formen von Wasserbehandlungen, die meisten davon sind öffentlich. Die Badeanstalt im Freien ist mit Jacuzzi, Abkühlbecken und Wasserfall ausgestattet. Ein türkisches Hamam, eine schwedische Sauna und ein Endlos-Pool, um den ganzen Tag zu entspannen. Das Hotel liegt auf Belle Isle, weit weg von Miamis Party Szene.

01 | Bedroom with outdoor bathing area.

Schlafzimmer mit Freiluftbad.

02 | Sauna-style gate to treatment rooms.
Gang zum Spa im Sauna-Look.

03 04
05

06

03 | Water treatment rooms.
Die Räumlichkeiten des Spas.

04 | Communal bathing area.
Öffentlicher Badeort.

05 | Lounge.
Lounge.

06 | Infinity pool.
Endlos-Pool.

hotel qt | new york city . new york
DESIGN: Lindy Roy

Hotelier André Balazs, behind such notorious projects as the Mercer Hotel and Standard Hotels, has teamed up with architect Lindy Roy and her firm Roy Co. for his outpost secretly nestled around the corner from Times Square. After searching out the hotel's orange sign on 45th Street, guests enter through a revolving door bathed in pink light and are greeted by a newsstand-cum-concierge desk in the lobby. Burrowing through a series of cavernous public spaces reveals retro chic interiors that transplant guests into a sixties-chalet in the middle of Manhattan. Voyeurs rejoice with glass partitions that separate the lobby from an in situ pool surrounded by an intimate bar and lounge. A DJ spins nightly from inside the cedar-walled poolroom and sauna filled with semi-clad beauties taking dips and lounging in the steam room. Because the hotel was converted from a 15-story office building, spaces are generally small, but replete with uniquely custom furnishings. Guestrooms are ingeniously filled with platform beds and bunk beds, mobile tables, reading lamps, and flat-screen TVs. Think of Hotel QT as an urban camp ground for those who pack their hairdryers and laptops for any outing.

Für dieses Hotel, das sich in einer entlegenen Ecke beim Times Square befindet, hat sich Hotelier André Balazs, der hinter so bekannten Projekten wie dem Mercer Hotel und Standard Hotels steht, mit der Architektin Lindy Roy und deren Firma Roy Co. zusammen getan. Nachdem der Gast das orangefarbene Hotelschild in der 45. Straße ausfindig gemacht hat, betritt er die Lobby durch eine in pinkfarbenes Licht getauchte Drehtür und wird am Empfang, der gleichzeitig als Kiosk dient, begrüßt. Beim Gang durch eine Reihe von öffentlichen Nischenplätzen entdeckt man die stylische Retro-Inneneinrichtung, die den Hotelgast in ein 60er-Jahre-Chalet im Herzen von Manhattan versetzt. Voyeure haben ihre Freude an den gläsernen Trennwänden, die die Lobby von einem Pool mit intimer Bar und Lounge abtrennen. Jede Nacht legt ein DJ innerhalb des mit Kiefernholz verkleideten Poolraums und der Sauna auf, während spärlich bekleidete Schönheiten in den Pool springen oder im Dampfbad relaxen. Da das Hotel aus einem 15-stöckigen Bürogebäude entstand, sind die Räume meist klein, doch mit einzigartigem Mobiliar ausgestattet. In den Gästezimmern finden sich Hoch- und Etagenbetten, Rolltische, Leselampen und Fernseher mit Flachbildschirmen. Das Hotel QT stellt man sich am besten als urbanen Campingplatz vor, für Menschen, die nie ohne Fön und Laptop aus dem Haus gehen.

01 | Swim up to the lobby's bar from the pool for some wet inebriation.

Vom Pool kann man zur Bar in der Hotellobby schwimmen und dort einen kühlen Drink zu sich nehmen.

02 | Swelter in the sauna's steam room and then cool off in the
neighboring shower.

Schwitzen Sie in der Dampfsauna und kühlen Sie sich danach
unter der Dusche ab.

03 | Bunk beds float above platform beds to make for a cosy
threesome.

Über den Doppelbetten schweben Hochbetten und sorgen für
eine behagliche Atmosphäre.

03

hotel on rivington | new york city . new york

DESIGN: India Mahdavi, Zaha Hadid

Originally home to tenements, delicatessens, and synagogues, the Lower East Side's recent urban regeneration has been catalyzed by up and comers Matthew Grzywinski and Amador Pons of Grzywinski Pons Architects and their luminous 21-story glass-and-aluminum tower. The soaring façade is clad with alternating pains of transparent and frosted glass that translate on the interior to light-filled guestrooms furnished by Paris-based designer India Mahdavi. Once inside you can expose what you like with the lights on, or pull back the curtains to find some repose in the dark from the teeming streets below. Exhibitionists can relax on balconies with sprawling views of fire escapes or get wet inside glass-encased steam showers. After shadow dancing in your room and ready to face the masses, saunter downstairs to chef Kurt Gutenbrunner's ground-floor restaurant, Thor, whose name is an acronym derived from that of the hotel. Marcel Walder's wallpaper-clad dining room boasts a 21-foot glass atrium with views of an historic tenement next door.

Ursprünglich bestand die Lower East Side hauptsächlich aus Mietshäusern, Feinkostgeschäften und Synagogen: Ihre urbane Neugestaltung wurde durch Matthew Grzywinski und Amador Pons von Grzywinski Pons Architekten mit ihrem glänzenden 21-stöckigem Turm aus Glas und Aluminium in Gang gesetzt. Die hoch aufragende Fassade ist mit Fensterscheiben aus transparentem und gefrostetem Glas versehen, welche die von der Pariser Designerin India Mahdavi ausgestatteten Gästezimmer mit Licht durchfluten. Im Innern kann man entweder alles in künstliches Licht tauchen oder einfach die Vorhänge zuziehen, um sich im Dunkeln von dem hektischen Betrieb auf den Straßen zu erholen. Freiluftfanatiker können sich auf den Balkonen mit Blick auf die überall verstreuten Feuertreppen entspannen oder sich in den gläsernen Dampfduschkabinen erfrischen. Wenn man dann wieder bereit ist, sich unter die Massen zu stürzen, dann kann man im Erdgeschoss Kurt Gutenbrunners Restaurant Thor einen Besuch abstatten (der Name ist ein Akronym, abgeleitet von dem des Hotels). Marcel Walders mit Tapeten ausgekleideter Speiseraum besitzt ein circa sechs Meter langes Glasatrium mit Ausblick auf ein historisches Wohnhaus.

01 | Guestrooms feature floor to ceiling windows with rambling views of the Lower East Side and Financial District.

Die Gästezimmer besitzen raumhohe Fenster mit einer weitläufigen Aussicht auf die Lower East Side und den Financial District.

02 | 03 | 04 Paris-based designer India
Mahdavi furnished each room and the
lobby with cool modernist flair.

Die in Paris lebende Designerin India
Mahdavi hat alle Zimmer und die
Lobby mit coolem, modernen Mobiliar
ausgestattet.

05 | Party 24/7 in the hotel's lounging lobby.

In der Hotel Lounge ist 24 Stunden
täglich Party.

hotel básico | playa del carmen . mexico

DESIGN: Moisés Isón, José Antonio Sánchez from Central de Arquitectura, Héctor Galván from omelette Interior Design

Even though the name promises a minimal esthetic, the hotel is anything but. Rather, it uses everyday industrial materials to create a pared-down but still visually vibrant environment. The designer took everyday objects and situations and used them in a stylish and unconventional way. The open-kitchen restaurant has the look and atmosphere of a local market stand where guests can choose their fish and vegetables that will become their dinner. The reception area doubles as a store and a fruit juice bar. The bare concrete walls of the rooms, reminiscent of a parking garage, achieve gallery-like chic with exposed plumbing fixtures and inner tubes. Basically, it looks like an art director designed a surfer hotel in the perfect world of a movie set. The roof deck is a lively bar area with two petroleum water tanks that are used as "pools", too small to swim in but nice to cool off in. Even though the ocean is just a few steps away, the hotel is where the party is. Flat screen TV's will screen the views of the ocean right into your room, giving new meaning to "ocean view room".

Obwohl der Name eine reduzierte, minimalistische Ästhetik vermuten lässt, ist dieses Hotel alles andere als das. Stattdessen werden industrielle Materialien benutzt um eine einfache aber lebendige Stimmung zu schaffen. Die Designer verwendeten alltägliche Gebrauchsgegenstände und setzten sie in unkonventioneller Weise ein. Die offene Restaurantküche ähnelt einem dörflichen Marktstand, in dem die Gäste ihren Fisch und das Gemüse aussuchen können, bevor es zubereitet wird. Die Rezeption ist zugleich ein Kolonialwarenladen und eine Obstsaft-Bar. Die kahlen Betonwände der Zimmer verlieren ihren Parkgaragencharakter durch sichtbare Leitungen, Wasserrohre und Schwimmringe, die wie Ausstellungsstücke an Galeriewänden platziert sind. Alles in allem sieht es aus, als hätte ein Set-Designer ein Surfer-Hotel für einen Film entworfen. Die Dachterrasse ist eine laute und lebendige Bar mit zwei großen Wassertrommeln, die als Planschbecken benutzt werden: Zu klein zum Schwimmen aber perfekt zum Abkühlen. Obwohl das Meer nur einige Schritte entfernt ist, geht definitiv hier die Post ab. Zudem bringen die Plasma-TVs die Wellen vor der Tür direkt in die Zimmer – eine neue Version von „Meerblick".

01 | Rooftop pools, former petroleum tanks overlooking the ocean.

Die Pools auf dem Dach – ehemalige Öltanks – mit Meeresblick.

02

02 | Patio restaurant serving fresh local seafood.

Im Terrassen-Restaurant werden frische Meeresfrüchte serviert.

03 | Most of the interior design uses recycled materials, paint, cotton and even latex.

Beim Innendesign wurden hauptsächlich Recycling-Materialien, Farbe, Baumwolle und sogar Latex verwendet.

05 | **06**

04 | The basic concepts and strong local identity are even reflected in the guestroom with the freestanding tub.

Grundkonzepte und die ausgeprägte Standortbezogenheit spiegeln sich auch im Gästezimmer mit freistehender Badewanne wider.

05 | Made out of a mixture of concrete and Caribbean sand, the building blends with the local beach atmosphere.

Das aus einer Beton-/Karibiksand-Mischung erbaute Gebäude verschmilzt mit der örtlichen Strandatmosphäre.

06 | The Bar La Azotea, on the 3rd floor rooftop offers cabanas made from the front of old trucks, a perfect view of the Caribbean and more.

Die Bar La Azotea auf der 3. Etage bietet aus LKW-Fronten hergestellte Cabanas, eine überwältigende Aussicht auf das Meer und noch vieles mehr.

1555 malabia house | buenos aires . argentina
DESIGN: Maria Bautista

The most exciting places in this world are the ones that have a story to tell. The 1555 Malabia House is just such a place. Built at the end of the 19th century, it first housed the women's home "Hogar de Señoras San Vicente Ferrer". A French benefactress had donated the property to a church. To this day, the Malabia House has remained a place of refuge – albeit in a positive sense. People who come here find exactly what they are looking for, no matter whether it is tranquillity or the excitement of Argentinean life. After all, owner Maria Bautista has made it her goal to present to her guests all facets of her Argentina. These facets especially include the beauty of the South American country and the flair of the city of Buenos Aires. Before Maria Bautista opened 1555 Malabia House in July of 1998, she had formed a clear idea of how the historical building was to eventually look. Without further ado, she took control with regard to design, thus ensuring that the house would become Argentina's first design Bed and Breakfast. Characteristic is the unique mix of styles, which combines European design with the Argentinean zest for life. The rooms, flooded with light, thus have an especially personal atmosphere and communicate a feeling of having arrived. Just as inviting is the quarter in which the Malabia House is situated: Palermo Viejo is among the most exclusive quarters of the Argentinean capital. Galleries, design and fashion shops, together with the typical tango bars, characterize the scene on the streets.

Die spannendsten Orte dieser Welt sind die, die etwas zu erzählen haben. Das 1555 Malabia House ist genau so ein Ort. Ende des 19. Jahrhunderts erbaut, beherbergte es zunächst das Frauenheim „Hogar de Señoras San Vicente Ferrer". Eine französische Wohltäterin hatte das Gelände einer Kirche gespendet. Das Malabia House ist bis heute ein Zufluchtsort geblieben – allerdings im positiven Sinn. Wer hierher kommt, findet das, wonach er sucht. Egal, ob es Ruhe oder das pralle argentinische Leben ist. Schließlich hat sich Eigentümerin Maria Bautista zum Ziel gesetzt, den Gästen alle Facetten ihres Argentiniens zu präsentieren. Eine besondere Rolle spielt dabei die Schönheit des südamerikanischen Landes und das Flair der Stadt Buenos Aires. Bevor Maria Bautista im Juli 1998 das 1555 Malabia House eröffnete, hatte sie genaue Vorstellungen, wie das historische Gebäude einmal aussehen sollte. Kurzerhand übernahm sie die Regie in punkto Design und sorgte so dafür, dass das Haus zum ersten Design Bed and Breakfast in Argentinien wurde. Kennzeichnend ist ein individueller Stilmix, der europäisches Design mit argentinischer Lebensfreude verbindet. Die lichtdurchfluteten Räume wirken so besonders persönlich und vermitteln das Gefühl angekommen zu sein. Genauso einladend ist das Viertel, in dem das Malabia House steht: Palermo Viejo gehört zu den exklusivsten Stadtteilen der argentinischen Hauptstadt. Galerien, Design- und Modegeschäfte prägen zusammen mit den typischen Tangobars das Straßenbild.

01 | The uniquely furnished rooms of 1555 Malabia House can house
a maximum of 33 guests.

Maximal 33 Gäste finden in den individuell eingerichteten
Zimmern des 1555 Malabia Houses Platz.

02 | The design concept follows the architecture of the building, erected over a hundred years ago.

Das Designkonzept folgt der Architektur des über hundert Jahre alten Gebäudes.

03 | The hotel's own library is a favourite spot of many guests.

Die hauseigene Bibliothek gehört zu den Lieblingsplätzen vieler Gäste.

portinari design hotel | rio de janeiro . brazil

DESIGN: Stella Orleans e Brangança, Luiz Fernando Redó, Gilmar Peres, Marcia Muller, Hélio Fraga, Luiz Fernando Grabowsky, Cadas Abranches, Gustavo and Sandra Pena, Chicô Gouveia

Rio de Janeiro is a city like a painting. Glistening waves and snow-white sand in the foreground, behind with an impressive skyline stretching across the outline of the brilliant green of the rainforest and the distinct silhouette of Sugar Loaf Mountain. It is precisely this image that the Brazilian painter Cândido Portinari had before his eyes for his entire life. Until his death in 1962, he dealt in an ever more expressionistic way with the theme of Brazilian life, and in doing so, became internationally famous. Thus, it is no wonder that the first Design Hotel in Brazil's capital not only bears Portinari's name, but is also dedicated to art. For instance, the twelve floors of the hotel, opened in 2003, were designed by various Brazilian artists. Among them are Luiz Fernando Grabowsky and Hélio Fraga. All of them based their creations on their own personal design concept. A few rooms are characterized by the interplay of light and shadow; in others, the focus is on natural materials or the use of traditional Brazilian patterns. Yet all 66 rooms and suites have one thing in common—the luxurious basic furnishings. Those who wish to not only look but actually plunge into South American life can access the most famous beach in Rio, the Copacabana, just a few steps away from the Portinari. There, every visitor can experience his or her own personal Brazilian carnival, live and at any time of the year.

Rio de Janeiro ist eine Stadt wie gemalt. Glitzernde Wellen und schneeweißer Sand im Vordergrund, dahinter eine beeindruckende Skyline, die sich vor dem leuchtenden Grün des Regenwalds und der markanten Silhouette des Zuckerhuts abzeichnet. Genau dieses Motiv hatte der brasilianische Maler Cândido Portinari ein Leben lang vor Augen. Bis zu seinem Tod 1962 beschäftigte er sich auf immer expressionistischere Weise mit dem brasilianischen Leben und wurde damit weltberühmt. Kein Wunder also, dass das erste Designhotel der Hauptstadt Brasiliens nicht nur den Namen Portinari trägt, sondern sich auch der Kunst verschrieben hat. So wurden die zwölf Etagen des 2003 eröffneten Hotels von verschiedenen brasilianischen Künstlern designt. Dazu gehören Luiz Fernando Grabowsky und Hélio Fraga. Alle legten ihr ganz persönliches Designkonzept bei der Gestaltung zugrunde. Einige Räume sind vom Zusammenspiel zwischen Licht und Schatten bestimmt, bei anderen liegt der Schwerpunkt auf Naturmaterialien oder dem Einsatz traditioneller brasilianischer Muster. Eins haben allerdings alle 66 Zimmer und Suiten gemeinsam – die luxuriöse Grundausstattung. Wer nicht nur schauen, sondern auch ins südamerikanische Leben eintauchen möchte, ist vom Portinari in wenigen Schritten am berühmtesten Strand Rios, der Copacabana. Dort kann dann jeder Besucher seinen persönlichen brasilianischen Karneval live erleben und zwar zu jeder Jahreszeit.

01 | 44 Deluxe rooms, eleven junior suites and eleven executive suites are housed in the Portinari Design Hotel.

44 Deluxe Zimmer, elf Junior Suiten und elf Executive Suiten gibt es im Portinari Design Hotel.

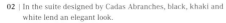

02 | In the suite designed by Cadas Abranches, black, khaki and white lend an elegant look.

In der von Cadas Abranches gestalteten Suite sorgen Schwarz, Khaki und Weiß für eine elegante Optik.

03 | Designers Gustavo and Sandra Pena designed all of the rooms on the second floor.

Die Designer Gustavo und Sandra Pena haben sämtliche Räume im zweiten Stock entworfen.

04 | Painter Cândido Portinari's presence in the Design Hotel is also evident in his pictures on its dinnerware.

Maler Cândido Portinari ist mit seinen Bildern auch auf dem Geschirr des Design Hotels präsent.

05 | In addition to generously planned bathrooms, the suites have their own sauna.

Neben großzügig geschnittenen Badezimmern haben die Suiten eine eigene Sauna.

normandie design hotel | são paulo . brazil

DESIGN: Edmundo Reinhold, Leonardo Manceñido

Based on the design concept of French designer Philippe Starck, the two Brazilians Edmundo Reinhold and Leonardo Manceñido have created a hotel atmosphere of minimalist elegance. In contrast to the loud, colorful and often hot and humid environment of the city, the 174-bed hotel is a refuge of tranquility in every sense of the word. The walls, all in white, the floors, ceilings and the color contrast of the furniture, reduced to black and white, generate an atmosphere of clarity and subtle understatement. Smooth materials such as leather, glass and black wenge wood reinforce this atmosphere. Several pieces of furniture, especially chairs and easy chairs, bear the name of famous designers such as Marcel Breuer or Charles Eames. Thanks to its optimal connections to public transportation, the hotel is not only a site for city tourists, but also ideal for business travelers. All suites and studios provide ample room for a work area, equipped with the most modern of media and communications technologies. Two conference rooms and a screening room offer the best conditions for conferences and conventions.

In Anlehnung an das Design-Konzept des Franzosen Philippe Starck haben die beiden Brasilianer Edmundo Reinhold und Leonardo Manceñido ein Hotelambiente von minimalistischer Eleganz geschaffen. Im Gegensatz zur lärmenden, bunten und oft schwül-heißen Umgebung der Metropole ist das 174-Betten-Haus ein Ruhepol in jeglicher Hinsicht. Die ganz in Weiß gehaltenen Wände, Fußböden, Decken und der auf schwarz-weiß reduzierte Farbkontrast des Mobiliars erzeugen eine Atmosphäre von Klarheit und dezentem Understatement. Glatte Materialien wie Leder, Glas oder schwarzes Wengeholz verstärken diese Atmosphäre. Etliche Möbelstücke, vor allem Stühle und Sessel, tragen den Namen bekannter Designer wie Marcel Breuer oder Charles Eames. Das Hotel ist dank seiner guten Anbindung an den öffentlichen Nahverkehr nicht nur optimaler Standort für Stadttouristen, sondern eignet sich auch für Geschäftsleute. Alle Suiten und Studios geben Raum genug für einen Arbeitsbereich, ausgestattet mit modernster Medien- und Kommunikationstechnik. Zwei Konferenzräume und ein Kinoraum bieten für Tagungen und Konferenzen beste Voraussetzungen.

01 | The color white is a thread throughout the hotel.
Die Farbe Weiß zieht sich wie ein roter Faden durch das Hotel.

02 | A strict black and white contrast dominates the room furnishings.

Beim Mobiliar der Zimmer dominiert der strenge Schwarz-Weiß-Kontrast.

03 | The restaurant–minimalist in design, exquisite in cuisine.

Das Restaurant – minimalistisch im Design, exquisit in der Küche.

04 | The lobby with chairs by Marcel Breuer and a fireplace for those rare cool days.

Die Lobby mit Stühlen von Marcel Breuer und einem Kamin für die seltenen kühlen Tage.

hotel index

Country / Location		Address	Information	Architecture & Design	Page
Great Britain	London	B+B Belgravia 64-66 Ebury Street Belgravia London, SW 1W 9QD UK www.bb-belgravia.com	opened 2004 17 rooms with free internet access, communal lounge area with open fire and large flat screen TV, all prices include full breakfast, 5 minutes to Victoria Train Station.	Lynne Reid	8
Belgium	Antwerp	Hotel Julien Korte Nieuwstraat 24 2000 Antwerpen Belgium www.hotel-julien.com	opened 2001 11 rooms housed in 2 entirely renovated historic houses, bar.	AID Architecten Kristl Bakermans Mouche Van Hool	12
Netherlands	Amsterdam	Hotel V Victorieplein 42 1078 PH Amsterdam Netherlands www.hotelv.nl	opened 2006 24 rooms, lobby, lounge, in-house wireless network, hotel garden, all prices include breakfast, located near congress center RAI in the southern part of Amsterdam, 5 taxi minutes to the center.	Mirjam Espinosa Ronald Hooft Consulting	16
Netherlands	Rotterdam	Stroom Lloydstraat 1 3024 EA Rotterdam Netherlands www.stroomrotterdam.nl	opened 2005 18 studios, bar, lounge, rooftop, gym.	Gerben van der Molen from Stars Design	20
Germany	Hamburg	25hours Paul-Dessau-Str. 2 22761 Hamburg Altona Germany www.25hours-hotel.de	opened 2003 89 rooms, 3 studios, living-room, 2 conference rooms, bar restaurant, located in the western part of Hamburg, 5 minutes to city center by car.	Thomas Lau, Mark Hendrik Blieffert from HPV Hamburg Evi Märklstetter, Armin Fischer from 3Meta	24

hotel index

hotel index

Country / Location		Address	Information	Architecture & Design	Page
Spain	Madrid	De las Letras Hotel & Restaurante Gran Vía n. 11 28013 Madrid Spain www.hoteldelasletras.com	opened 2005 103 rooms, some of them with solarium terraces and jacuzzi on the terrace, restaurant and lounge, summer terrace in the penthouse, spa, jacuzzi, hamam, sauna, massage rooms, library, located in the center, few minutes to theaters, cinemas and shopping.	Virginia Figueras	48
France	Paris	Little Palace Hôtel 4, rue Salomon de Caus F-75003 Paris France www.littlepalacehotel.com	renovated 2005 built in the beginning of the century 49 rooms (standard, superior), 4 suites, restaurant, bar, located in the center of Paris next to the main tourist places and business districts.	Cabinet Interieur Design	52
Italy	Florence	Una Hotel Vittoria Via Pisana, 59 50143 Florence Italy www.unahotels.it/english/ hotels/vittoria.htm	opened 2003 84 rooms, bar, restaurant, conference rooms, located in historical quarter of San Frediano, near the Lungarno.	Fabio Novembre	56
Italy	Milan	Enterprise Hotel Corso Sempione 91 20154 Milan Italy www.enterprisehotel.com	opened 2002 123 rooms, 6 junior suites, 2 suites, lounge, day offices, restaurant, garden bar, congress center with newest audio-visual devices, close to the Fair of Milan and downtown.	Sofia Gioia Vedani Christina di Carlo Christopher Redfern	60
Greece	Mykonos	Theoxenia 84600 Kato Mili Mykonos Greece www.mykonostheoxenia.com	opened 2004 52 rooms and suites, few minutes to the nightlife of Mykonos town and shopping streets, 5 minutes drive from the airport and port.	Angelos Angelopoulos The Late Aris Constantinides Yiannis Tsimas	64

hotel index

Country / Location		Address	Information	Architecture & Design	Page
Turkey	Istanbul	Sumahan on the Water Kuleli caddesi no: 51 Cengelköy 34684 Istanbul Turkey www.sumahan.com	opened 2005 6 deluxe, 3 junior suites, 4 loft suites, 3 family loft suites, 2 execu- tive suites, library, restaurant, café bar, meeting facilities, located in Cengelköy, village of wooden houses, hotel on the water, seascape view from every bedroom.	Yasha Savcan Butler Nedret Tayyibe Butler Mark Horne Butler	70
Morocco	Essaioura	Madada Mogador 5, rue Youssef el fassi 44000 Essaouira Morocco www.madada.com	opened 2004 5 rooms, 1 suite, terrace on roof top, restaurant, overlooking the harbor and beaches, some steps to the ocean, 6 km to Essaioura Airport.	Jonathan Amar	76
Morocco	Marrakesh	Caravanserai 264 Ouled Ben Rahmoun Marrakesch Morocco www.caravanserai.com	opened 2001 8 rooms, 12 suites, restaurant, swimming pool, garden, large fireplace, hamam, 15 minutes from the center of Marrakesch.	Mathieu Boccara Max Lawrence	80
South Africa	Cape Town	Jardin D'ébène 21 Warren Street Tamboerskloof Cape Town, 8001 South Africa www.jardindebene.co.za	opened 2004 4 rooms, lounge space right next to plunge pool, in the heart of the City Bowl, right below Table Mountain, ten minutes drive from the beach.	Pascale Lauber Ulrike Bauschke	84
Hong Kong	Hong Kong	JIA Hong Kong 1-5 Irving Street Causeway Bay Hong Kong www.jiahongkong.com	opened 2004 54 studios and suites including two 1570 square feet penthouses on 24 floors, all rooms with fully equipped kitchen, open-air podium and sundeck on the 2nd floor, restaurant/ lounge, conference room, located in the Causeway Bay district.	Philippe Starck	88

hotel index

hotel index

hotel index

Country / Location	Address	Information	Architecture & Design	Page
New York New York City	Hotel on Rivington 107 Rivington Street New York New York, 10002 USA www.hotelonrivington.com	opened 2004 91 rooms and 19 suites including one Penthouse Suite, all rooms and suites with floor to ceiling glass walls and city views, private terraces, in-room spa services, situated in Manhattan on the Lower East Side, walking distance to Tribeca and Soho.	India Mahdavi Zaha Hadid	138
Mexico Playa del Carmen	Hotel Básico 5ta. Avenida & Calle 10 Norte, Playa del Carmen Quintana Roo, C.P.77710 Mexico www.hotelbasico.com	opened 2005 15 rooms, including 3 suites, cocktail bar. first floor patio restaurant, bar on the rooftop terrace, near to restaurants, shops, bars, nightclubs and only a few steps away from the ocean, 40 minutes by car to Cancun Airport.	Moisés Isón and José Antonio Sánches from Central de Arquitectura Héctor Galván from omelette Interior Design	142
Argentina Buenos Aires	1555 Malabia House Malabia 1555 C1414 DME Palermo Viejo Soho Buenos Aires Argentina www.malabiahouse.com.ar	opened 1998 12 superior rooms with own bathrooms, 3 standard and 1 balcony room with shared bathrooms, reading rooms, central patio, meeting facilities.	Maria Bautista	148
Brazil Rio de Janeiro	Portinari Design Hotel Rua Francisco Sá 17 Posto 6, Copacabana Rio de Janeiro Brazil www.hotelportinari.com.br	opened 2003 66 rooms on 11 floors, 44 Deluxe rooms; 11 Junior Suites and 11 Executive Suites, Brodowski Restaurant and bar on rooftop, one block from Copacabana Beach.	Stella Orleans e Bragança, Luiz Fernando Redó, Gilmar Peres, Marcia Muller, Hélio Fraga, Luiz Fernando Grabowsky, Cadas Abranches, Gustavo and Sandra Pena, Chicô Gouveia	152
Brazil São Paulo	Normandie Design Hotel Av. Ipiranga 1187 São Paulo Brazil www.normandiedesign.com.br	opened 1983 174 rooms including 10 suites and 15 Design Studios, restaurant, lobby bar with fireplace, conference facilities located downtown, close to the most important historical and cultural monuments, within walking distance to seven subway stations.	Leonardo Manceñido Edmundo Reinhold	156

architects & designers

photo credits

all other photos by Roland Bauer and Martin Nicholas Kunz

imprint

Bibliographic information published by Die Deutsche Bibliothek. Die Deutsche Bibliothek lists this publication in the Deutsche Nationalbibliografie; detailed bibliographic data are available on the internet at http://ddb.de

ISBN 10: 3-89986-070-5

ISBN 13: 978-3-89986-070-2

1st edition

© 2006 Martin Nicholas Kunz

© 2006 fusion publishing gmbh, stuttgart . los angeles

© 2006 avedition GmbH, Ludwigsburg

Printed in Austria

by Vorarlberger Verlagsanstalt AG, Dornbirn

Editors | Martin Nicholas Kunz, Patricia Massó

Editorial coordination | Hanna Martin

Copy editing | Rosina Geiger

Translations | Ade Team, Dr. Andrea Adelung

Layout | Hanna Martin, Alexander Storck

Imaging | Jan Hausberg

avedition GmbH

Königsallee 57 | 71638 Ludwigsburg | Germany

p +49-7141-1477391 | f +49-7141-1477399

www.avedition.com | kontakt@avedition.com

Further information and links at

www.bestdesigned.com

www.fusion-publishing.com

Texts (pages) | Frank Bantle (32, 70), Frank Deppe (24, 44, 76), Marei Drassdo (28, 156), Jaenette Drauwe (48, 98), Bärbel Holzberg (36, 40), Martin Nicholas Kunz (12), Karin Mahle (106, 112, 116, 120, 124, 128, 142), Erika Ranft (60, 84), Carolin Schöngarth (introduction, 8, 16, 20, 56, 80, 88, 92, 102, 148, 152), Heinfried Tacke (52, 64), Sean Weiss (134, 138)

Special thanks to Rob Alleman, Élan Hotel Modern | Ulrike Bauschke, Jardin D'ébène | Elena Boldrini, Una Hotels | Penny Brown, B+B Belgravia | Jörn-Carsten Bube, Hopper St. Antonius | Marc and Nedret Butler, Sumahan on the Water | Christine Dadda, Madada Mogador | Leonor Dietrich, Normandie Design Hotel | Marc Engler, Hotel Bristol | Mirjam Espinosa, Hotel V | Ulrike Fohr, 25hours | Sheeva Harilela, JIA Hong Kong | Dorna Hekmat, Cortiina | Robert Hollmann, Hollmann Beletage | Mouche Van Hool, Hotel Julien | Pacha Jahlan, Madada Mogador | Michel Kolenbrander, Stroom | Pascale Lauber, Jardin D'ébène | Charalambos Lardas, Theoxenia | Ariel Lu, United Hotel | Adil Mghinia, Caravanserai | Rafael Micha, Grupo HABITA | Jorge Moreno Sánchez, Habitat Hotels | Katie Oakley, The Prince | Yvonne Ongpin, The Mosser | Ellen Picataggio, The Farmer's Daughter | Paola Picollo, Enterprise Hotel | Pablo S. Piglia, 1555 Malabia House | Sonia Rosa, Enterprise Hotel | Alejandro Rueda, Hotel Básico | Philippe Santerre, Little Palace Hôtel | Dawn Shalhoup, Hotel Adagio | Cristian Tarrasco, Banys Orientals | Michael Tavani, Nadine Johnson PR | Melissa Vree, The Mosser | Sharon Vu, M Hotel Singapore | Tammy Walker, Becca PR | Angélique Weiss, Portinari Design Hotel for their support

Martin Nicholas Kunz

1957 born in Hollywood. Founder of fusion publishing creating content for architecture, design, travel, and lifestyle publications.

Patricia Massó

1962 born in Stuttgart. Working as marketing and PR consultant with an emphasis on hotel business and editor of several hotel and design books.

best designed:

outdoor living

modular houses

hotel pools

best designed hotels:

asia pacific

americas

europe I (urban)

europe II (countryside)

best designed wellness hotels:

asia pacific

americas

europe

africa & middle east

All books are released in German and English